FROM
ASESSIPPI
TO ZED LAKE

FROM ASESSIPPI TO ZED LAKE

A GUIDE TO MANITOBA'S PROVINCIAL PARKS

TEXT BY SHELLEY PENZIWOL
PHOTOGRAPHY BY PETER BLAHUT

GREAT PLAINS
PUBLICATIONS

Great Plains Publications
345-955 Portage Avenue
Winnipeg, MB R3G 0P9
www.greatplains.mb.ca

Great Plains Publications gratefully acknowledges the financial support
provided for its publishing program by the Government of Canada through
the Canada Book Fund; the Canada Council for the Arts; the Province of
Manitoba through the Book Publishing Tax Credit and the Book Publisher
Marketing Assistance Program; and the Manitoba Arts Council.

Design & Typography by Relish Design Studio Inc.
Printed in Canada by Friesens

Library and Archives Canada Cataloguing in Publication

Penziwol, Shelley

 From Asessippi to Zed Lake : a guide to Manitoba's provincial
parks / Shelley Penziwol ; photography by Peter Blahut.

Includes bibliographical references and index.

ISBN 978-1-926531-14-4

 1. Parks--Manitoba. 2. Manitoba--Description and travel.
I. Blahut, Peter II. Title.

FC3363.P46 2011 333.78'3097127 C2011-901854-3

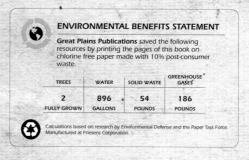

ENVIRONMENTAL BENEFITS STATEMENT

Great Plains Publications saved the following
resources by printing the pages of this book on
chlorine free paper made with 10% post-consumer
waste.

TREES	WATER	SOLID WASTE	GREENHOUSE* GASES
2 FULLY GROWN	896 GALLONS	54 POUNDS	186 POUNDS

Calculations based on research by Environmental Defense and the Paper Task Force.
Manufactured at Friesens Corporation

Acknowledgements

Many people deserve credit for their assistance in providing information and feedback as this book was coming together. From the Parks and Natural Areas Branch of Manitoba Conservation, thanks to Barry Bentham, Elisabeth Ostrop, and Morgan Hallett, and from the Regional Services and Parks Division of Manitoba Conservation, thanks to Sue Atkin, Bob Bomberak, Jim Johnson, Rod MacCharles, Bruce Mineault, and Madelyn Robinson. Also many thanks to Paul Deneer from Manitoba Conservation's office in Swan River for guidance into Kettle Stones. For assistance in locating historical details, thanks to staff at the Legislative Library, and to Wendy Barber and Marvyl Ginter at the Conservation Library. For providing extra photos, thanks to the Parks and Natural Areas Branch, the Protected Areas Initiative, Dennis Fast, Vince Crichton, and Steven Wintemute. Lastly, a special 'thank you' to Jana Wenzel for the portrait photos.

Contents

Contents

Introduction

Everyone Needs a Little Recreation

Marvel at the stillness of a river, trees and sky reflected in the water as perfectly as the view on the far shore. Follow the river downstream, and watch the water tumble over picturesque falls and rapids; a sight and sound so mesmerizing it is hard to walk away. Find a shoreline facing west and watch the sun set, blazing a fiery trail across the waves. A perfect day that plays itself out in any number of Manitoba's 84 provincial parks.

Parks followed people, at least at first. Many decades before Manitoba's first Provincial Parks Act officially established the legislative framework for a network of provincial parks, Manitobans across the province sought and found many of the recreational hot spots we still visit today.

By the late nineteenth and early twentieth centuries, southern Manitoba was settled, an agricultural economy was burgeoning, and Winnipeg was fast becoming the centre of commerce and trade on the prairies. Winnipeggers in that era may have played in Assiniboine, Kildonan and many other city parks, but the growing population, spreading railways, and the emergence of the automobile meant that more people had the means to look farther afield for recreational opportunities. Everybody wants a little bit of recreation in their lives. Some looked to the forest, others to the prairie, still others to the lake.

By Rail and Water

Railways blazed the trail to early recreation destinations. The first train travelled the Canadian Pacific line between Winnipeg and Kenora, then known as Rat Portage, in 1882, and the Canadian National's line was built in the same vicinity just over 20 years later. By 1887 under the headline of "happy people," the *Manitoba Free Press* reported that "there has been an almost continuous rush of hot Winnipeggers in the direction of the cool shores and shady isles of the Lake of the Woods." The railway to Kenora carried travellers and railway employees through the heart of the Whiteshell. Within a few short decades, cottage lots were leased around Brereton, Nora, Florence, West Hawk, and Falcon lakes near the rail line.

The attraction of Lake of the Woods made many people consider local options in their own backyard. By 1891, a rail line was proposed between Winnipeg and Selkirk as Winnipeggers were "anxious for some place to have an outing — and they are beginning to realize that Rat Portage is too far away — it costs too

"In the case of country people, some of them had picnic sites, camp grounds, and summer places on various lakes and rivers throughout southern Manitoba before the turn of the 20th century. Some of these were situated at Max Lake in Turtle Mountain, at Rock, Pelican, and Killarney lakes, at Oak Lake, at the Little Saskatchewan near Minnedosa, at the great oxbow of the Assiniboine at Portage la Prairie, and at the Delta Beach on Lake Manitoba. At all these places, first used only for picnics, fishing, and shooting, summer homes were later built, and here the pattern of outdoor recreation in Manitoba became established at an early date."

—Charles T. Thomas, Manitoba Pageant, Winter 1970

much to go there — when they can have just as nice a resort at their own door."

Manitoba's lakes were in fact already drawing visitors. By 1893, the local newspaper reported that quite a number of Portage la Prairie residents were camping at Lake Manitoba. Also by the turn of the century steamboats carried travellers up Lake Winnipeg for "real holiday boat trips" to places such as Gull Harbour, Berens River and Norway House.

By the turn of the century, Lake Winnipeg with its long stretches of sandy beaches, was poised to become the new hot spot. Canadian Pacific moved up the west shore of Lake Winnipeg to Winnipeg Beach by 1903. Demand was impressive. Within a few years, 12 to 15 trains a day were carrying more than 40,000 passengers to Winnipeg Beach on summer holiday weekends. Canadian

Northern, later Canadian National, also saw the potential of Lake Winnipeg as a vacation destination, and in 1916 the first passenger train arrived in Grand Beach on the east side of the lake. That same year, the railway was extended to Victoria Beach. To entice visitors, the railways built hotels and other amusements, including the CPR's Empress Hotel in Winnipeg Beach and the CNR's Grand Beach Hotel. Private cottage communities were established in areas along the railroads.

In the Forest

The federal government began establishing forest reserves, withdrawing lands from sale, disposition or occupancy. Although often presumed that reserves were to preserve the forest, forest reserve lands were lands unsuitable for agricultural production, set aside permanently for lumber production. With forest reserve status, timber was protected to maintain a full and constant supply to meet the needs of the people in the surrounding areas. Forest reserves provided for a continued lumber industry. Spruce Woods, Turtle Mountain, and Riding Mountain Forest Reserves were established in 1895, followed in 1906 by Duck Mountain and Porcupine Forest Reserves. By 1915, the federal government began developing forest reserves for recreational purposes by constructing roads, campgrounds and picnic areas — uses that were not incompatible with the purpose of forest reserves.

In 1930, Riding Mountain Forest Reserve became Riding Mountain National Park, Manitoba's first national park. Upon its official opening in July 1933, Manitoba's lieutenant governor James McGregor wisely observed, "As time goes on and as our country becomes more populated, the value of these great public areas must increase. Long after those who have taken such an active part in the creation of Riding Mountain National Park have passed on, when our prairies are populated with millions, this park will remain an endearing and visible heritage of pioneer days. To the residents of Manitoba and to the generations to come I dedicate this park, a perpetual reminder of the right of people to the national ownership of regions of outstanding scenic beauty, an expression of our developing sense of national consciousness, and an evidence of our instinctive love of the land."

In 1930, The Natural Resources Transfer Act transferred the responsibility for natural resources, including forests, from the federal government to the provinces. This authority over its lands and forests gave Manitoba the ability to develop those areas, and it moved quickly by establishing the Whiteshell Forest Reserve in 1931, setting the stage for future provincial park development.

The Great Depression brought hardship and change to many Manitobans. But while fortunes and lives were altered by financial and climatic conditions, recreation development continued unabated. As part of the "Single Unemployed Men's Relief Commission," 300 men were put to work for three years. By 1932, campground and lot boundaries were surveyed at Falcon Lake, and at West Hawk and Caddy Lakes in 1933. These men planned and laid out roads and subdivisions and designed buildings. A second large relief camp was established on Duck Mountain to construct buildings, access roads and other work as part of creating a Forest Experimental Area near Singush Lake, retained by the Federal Government at the time of transfer.

Attention was turned elsewhere during the Second World War, and rationing of gasoline, tires and canned goods put a damper on travel. But keen interest in recreation and related development resumed in the post-war period. In 1946, the province speculated that "the end of the war and the consequent release of tension quite naturally resulted in turning of people's attention towards the peace of the woods and lakes and streams." The province responded to this interest by developing more campgrounds, picnic areas, and cottage subdivisions on Crown lands. Cormorant Forest Reserve northeast of The Pas was established in 1948, and Northwest Angle Forest Reserve was established in the extreme southeast of the province in 1956.

Highways to Adventure

Just as the railways opened access to Lakes Winnipeg and Manitoba and parts of the Whiteshell, highway and road construction created even more opportunities. In 1932 the section of the Trans-Canada Highway between Winnipeg and Kenora was completed, and by 1938 it was hard-surfaced. The highway (now called Highway 44) took drivers from Lockport through Garson, Beausejour, and Whitemouth, to Rennie, and through the Whiteshell and into Ontario. Work at clearing streets and lanes in Falcon Lake got underway in 1955. In 1956, hydroelectric power was extended to the area and amenities including a golf course and shopping centre followed.

On the other side of the province, Highway 10 reached The Pas in 1939 and Flin Flon in 1950. Billed the "high road to adventure", the highway connected Flin Flon and its surroundings through Brandon south to North Dakota.

With the construction of highways and roads throughout the province, the development of wayside parks followed. While travelling the highways of Manitoba, small parks provided welcome rest stops for drivers.

Park development was not limited to southern Manitoba. Regardless of location, recreational spots sprang up nearby. Within a few short years of the establishment of the mining community of Lynn Lake, for example, Zed Lake and Burge Lake parks were established for residents. The same occurred at Snow Lake with development at Wekusko Falls, Thompson, with development at Paint Lake, and even Bissett, with recreational development at Wallace Lake.

Becoming a Park

A park reserve is often, but not always, the precursor to a provincial park. Park reserve status provides interim protection for an area of land while it is being considered for inclusion in Manitoba's system of provincial parks. Park reserve status can last six months, or be extended for periods up to five years. Public consultation occurs during this time. Once the province is ready to move forward, the Lieutenant Governor in Council may, by regulation, designate lands as provincial parks.

Little Limestone Lake is a famous marl lake north of Grand Rapids near the northwestern tip of Lake Winnipeg. In a marl lake like Little Limestone, calcite precipitates from the water as water temperature rises, changing the lake's colour to various hues of blue throughout the day. Little Limestone Lake became a park reserve in July 2007 and its park reserve status was renewed in 2008 for a period of five years. Public consultations occurred in 2010.

In other situations, provincial parks can be established by statute. In June 2010, the Manitoba Legislature assented to *The Upper Fort Garry Heritage Provincial Park Act*. This act acknowledges the cultural and historical importance of Upper Fort Garry and provides for the establishment of the new park. The original Upper Fort Garry, located along present-day Main Street in Winnipeg just south of its intersection with Broadway, was constructed in 1836 and torn down in the 1880s. The Governor's Gate is all that remains. Upper Fort Garry will become a provincial park when the act is officially proclaimed.

Less Work, More Play

While development of railways, roads, and recreational facilities provided Manitobans with a recreational infrastructure to be used and enjoyed, the emergence of the five-day workweek in the 1940s, '50s and '60s meant that Manitobans could devote less time to work, and more time to recreational pursuits. Compulsory holiday periods, the two-day weekend, and "an unceasing public urge to vacation" created unprecedented demand for places to go and things to see.

By the mid-1950s, it was reported that "Manitobans, weary of the city streets and the noise of heavy traffic, are turning more and more to the province's beach resorts to spend long weekends and summer holidays." In the Whiteshell Forest Reserve, all tent and trailer campgrounds were filled to overflowing during the summer, available beaches were overcrowded on weekends and the demand for summer home lots was hardly met.

Parks, Officially

By 1939, the headline in the Winnipeg *Tribune* asked readers "Why Not Manitoba Parks?" The writer noted that Saskatchewan had seven parks, and Ontario, Quebec and British Columbia had several each. Manitoba had none, officially. The writer of the article noted that "the very term 'park' arouses interest at sight and suggests conveniences for the traveller, where 'forest reserve' is likely to suggest a closed area." The

following year, another article appeared in the *Tribune* reminding readers that Manitoba still had no provincial parks, and that it was missing out on the opportunity to advertise its scenic areas.

The government did advertise its scenic spots. The first illustrated booklet promoting the Whiteshell Forest Reserve was published in 1940, and numerous newspaper articles extolled the virtues of the area — "scenic wonders lure tourists to Whiteshell", "Whiteshell is fine heritage for Manitoba", and many others. And the forest reserve was called Whiteshell Provincial Park by many, including the government, even though the designation was unofficial.

Throughout the 1940s and '50s, recreation development was carried out by different parts of government, including the Forest Service, the Lands Branch, and Public Works. Large amounts of money were being spent in certain areas of the province, especially in the Whiteshell. It became obvious that coordination of efforts would be beneficial for ongoing management of the developed areas, as well as for future planning.

The first Provincial Parks Act was passed in the Manitoba Legislature in 1960. The act gave the minister of the Department of Mines and Natural Resources the responsibility to manage, operate, and develop parks "as to preserve to the greatest extent possible the value and use thereof for recreational purposes." A Parks Division had been formed in the Forest Service in 1959 to administer the legislation.

Perhaps best remembered for the construction of the Red River Floodway in the 1960s, Duff Roblin, Premier of Manitoba from 1958 to 1967 also established our province-wide parks system. Duff Roblin Provincial Park, located along the Red River Floodway, commemorates both accomplishments.

The Provincial Parks Act allowed for the designation in 1961 of four large parks including the Whiteshell, Turtle Mountain, Grand Beach and Duck Mountain, along with forty smaller recreation areas. The 1960s also saw the designation of many of the parks that are still popular recreation spots today — Clearwater Lake, Grass River, St. Malo, Asessippi, Birds Hill, Spruce Woods, and Hecla.

Parks Are Not Just For People

By the late 1960s, there was a shift in thinking that aligned with a corresponding growth in environmental awareness – parks were not just for personal consumption any longer. The Provincial Park Lands Act, passed in 1972 to replace the 1960 version, ensured that parks existed for Manitobans and visitors, but also could exist for conservation and management of plants and animals, and to preserve geological or cultural features. The first "system plan" for Manitoba's provincial parks was completed in 1983. It recognized the need for parks to represent all of the province's natural regions. The notion of a heritage park first emerged during this period. And Manitoba's first wilderness park, Atikaki, was designated in 1985.

In 1993, a new Provincial Parks Act replaced the 1972 version, and this law is still in place today. This version of the act redefined park classifications. Parks are now designated as recreation, natural, heritage or wilderness. The act also introduced land use categories that help to identify the main purpose of park lands. A park, for example, could (and often does) contain several land use categories that delineate areas used for recreation and development, from areas that protect natural landscapes, and from areas that preserve cultural and heritage aspects of the park.

Let the Journey Begin

Since 1961 when the first parks were established, Manitoba's system of parks has grown to include 84 parks, and it continues to grow, even as this book goes into publication. Surely the thought of 84 parks arouses curiosity. Perhaps it makes you mentally list the ones you have visited, or maybe if you are well-travelled there are too many to count in your head. Regardless, there are probably many that you have not seen, or not even recognized as being provincial parks.

So visit an old favourite, or find two or ten more. Stop along the

Parks as Home

About 6,200 cottages are located within provincial park boundaries, and over 600 of those have been declared as primary residences. People do not just cottage in provincial parks on weekends and in the summer — a growing number call parks home. Although provincial park residents do not pay municipal property taxes, they do pay something similar called a chief place residence levy along with other park service fees.

highway, or spend a day, or a week. Feel the spray of a waterfall, or a downtown fountain at lunch. Walk a path in the forest and take in the view from a look-out tower. Get up close and personal with a new sandy beach, a glacier-scoured chunk of granite warmed by the sun, or a carefully restored bit of prairie. Be lulled by loons and waves. Relax. Discover this province in ways you never thought you would. Every park has a story. Read on to discover some of them. ■

A to Z

Asessippi to Zed Lake

Asessippi

YOU HAVE GOT TO LOVE A PLACE THAT HAS INSPIRED ART, or at least be intrigued by it. Asessippi Provincial Park is located west of Riding Mountain National Park at the confluence of the Shell and Assiniboine Rivers. Not only is the park situated where two rivers meet, it is situated where two glacial river valleys meet — an even more incredible sight. As the last glacier melted over 10,000 years ago, torrents of water were carried in these large glacial spillways and channels before eventually flowing into Lake Agassiz. The huge volumes of water have long since disappeared, but the rolling prairie valleys that remain are no less impressive.

The construction of the Shellmouth Dam in the 1960s to control flooding downstream along the Assiniboine River created Lake of the Prairies, a 67-kilometre long "water conservation" reservoir now popular with anglers. The Shell River, with its origins in the Duck Mountains, flows into the Assiniboine River just upstream of the Shellmouth Dam. The

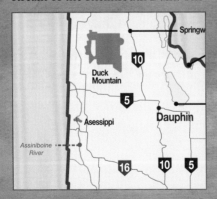

dam itself is located within the park and provides an interesting vantage point from which to view both valleys at the same time.

Shortly after Asessippi was designated a provincial park, the *Winnipeg Free Press* called Asessippi the "latest addition to the list of tongue-twisters among the provincial parks." To assist readers, it explained that Asessippi is pronounced much like Mississippi, except of course for the first syllable. The park was named after the community of Asessippi, first established in the Shell River valley in the early 1880s by the Shell River Colonization Company. Asessippi is the Cree name for Shell River. By 1883, about 50 immigrants from Ontario settled in Asessippi and the town soon boasted a grist mill, saw mill, shingle factory, brick works, cheese factory, and even a curling club. When an expected railway did not materialize, businesses closed and many in the community moved away. Within a few decades, Asessippi went from bustling prairie community to ghost town. Walk the Asessippi Village trail at the eastern edge of the park to visit the former townsite.

In 1903, the *Free Press* reported that one sanguine citizen had purchased the whole of Asessippi and all of the varied interests in the village including the mills, store, and other buildings. The writer further noted that "this place with splendid water privileges will be certain to attract another community." While perhaps not in the way the writer envisioned, the area's splendid water privileges did attract attention, eventually. Asessippi was designated a provincial park in 1964 and officially opened in 1973.

When the park's 23 square kilometre area of prairie and aspen forest was developed, park planners separated four main recreational areas to prevent interference between the areas. Four areas include a large boat launch near the dam, a day use area, a beach with nearby concessions, and a campground that today boasts over 100 basic and electrical campsites plus yurts. Many walking trails, including the Ancient Valley trail, allow visitors to explore the valleys' glacial origins. The Trans Canada Trail also crosses the park, entering the park along its eastern boundary, and exiting to the north.

The park is also home to the Asessippi Ski Area, a privately-operated resort located on the south side of the Shell River valley. It may not be the Rockies, but the terrain of the glacial Shell River valley and the mountain-village appearance of the resort gives the ski area an alpine atmosphere.

The "almost human forms" of Asessippi's hills influenced artist Don Proch, who was raised nearby. In 1972, a Winnipeg Art Gallery exhibit called *The Legend of Asessippi* included creative prairie-themed art by Proch and fellow artists. In 1975, Proch's WAG exhibit was titled *Asessippi Clouds.*

Entrance to the park is via Provincial Road 482, just west of Highway 83, the main highway running along the western edge of the province, connecting the communities of Roblin and Russell, and others. ∎

Asessippi

Atikaki

GORGEOUS EXPOSED ROCK OUTCROPS PAINTED BY ANCIENT PEOPLES, pristine wilderness rivers, and rich boreal forest can be found in this area that was once part of a mountain range formed billions of years ago when the earth was young, long since modified by glaciers and weather. Named for Boreas, the Greek god of the north wind, the boreal forest covers approximately one third of all wooded lands on the planet, and a significant portion of Manitoba. In 1985, Atikaki Provincial Park (pronounced a-tick-a-kee), 3981 square kilometres in size and set in the boreal forest of eastern Manitoba, became Manitoba's first wilderness park.

Manitoba Conservation, Protected Areas Initiative

Vince Crichton

On a map, Atikaki's boundaries extend along its major rivers like tentacles reaching for Lake Winnipeg.

True to its name, Atikaki, meaning "country of the caribou," is home to a few hundred woodland caribou. As they are seldom seen or heard, woodland caribou are often considered to be secretive animals. Caribou's lichen-rich diet includes reindeer moss and old man's beard that hangs from branches in mature forests. In spring, they often calve on the many islands in Sasaginnigak Lake, one of the largest lakes in the park. Woodland caribou is a threatened species in Manitoba, and there are far fewer of them compared to their barren ground caribou relatives in the north. To succeed, they require large tracts of undeveloped wilderness that is free from the kind of habitat destruction that results from forestry, mining, hydro, or even recreational, development.

Other than caribou, the park is best known for its selection of Manitoba's finest wilderness rivers. On a map, Atikaki's boundaries extend along its major rivers like tentacles reaching for Lake Winnipeg. Perhaps the most famous river, the Bloodvein, became Manitoba's first Canadian

Heritage River in 1987. "Effortless paddling and easy portages" along with spectacular scenery make the Bloodvein a favourite with canoeists. Other well-known rivers in the park include the Gammon, Leyond, and Pigeon.

Recognizing that ecosystems extend beyond borders, Atikaki is part of a 9,400 square kilometre Interprovincial Wilderness Area that includes Atikaki, parts of Nopiming, Ontario's Woodland Caribou Provincial Park and Ontario's Eagle-Snowshoe Conservation Reserve. Established by the governments of Manitoba and Ontario in 2008, the jurisdictions committed to working together to conserve the ecological integrity of the area. Atikaki is also included in the area called Pimachiowin Aki or "the land that gives life" that has been proposed as a UNESCO World Heritage Site.

Atikaki is not road-accessible, but there are several fly-in lodges and outcamps in the park. There are also several outfitters offering canoe adventures on Atikaki's rivers. ∎

Atikaki

Bakers Narrows

THE SHORE OF BEAUTIFUL LAKE ATHAPAPUSKOW, a lake that spans the boundary between the Precambrian Shield and the Manitoba Lowlands, is home to Bakers Narrows Provincial Park. Lake Athapapuskow, or Athapap for short, has been described as an ideal recreational destination with "exquisite scenery and many rocky islands to make sheltered water for boating and angling in almost any weather." The lake has three distinct parts. Bakers Narrows, believed to be named after a local miner, connects the north arm of the lake to its middle portion. Climb a lookout tower in the park for a bird's eye view of the surroundings and you will see why Athapapuskow in the Cree language means "rocks on both sides" or "rocks all around." On a clear day, you will also see the old smelter stack in nearby Flin Flon.

The history of Bakers Narrows Provincial Park is completely entwined with the history of Flin Flon as a mining community. The discovery in 1914 of an ore body marked the beginning of development in northwestern Manitoba. By 1915, the Flin Flon mining claim, named after Flintabbatty Flonatin, hero of a novel by J.E. Preston Muddock called The Sunless City, was staked. Initially, equipment and supplies were hauled over water between The Pas and the Flin Flon site. Hudson Bay Mining and Smelting was incorporated in 1927 and the railway reached Flin Flon by 1929. Highway 10 reached Flin Flon in 1950 and was officially opened in 1951 during the community's first annual trout festival.

The highway was instrumental in opening the area up to visitors, and many private tourist camps and lodges were established. By 1952, 8,000 people crowded Bakers

Narrows during the second annual trout festival, cheering on competitors in the gold rush canoe derby. Bakers Narrows became a provincial park in 1961. Today, the park — at 1.45 square kilometres in size — is still a popular day spot with picnic areas, beaches and boat launches. Bakers Narrows campground offers over 100 basic and electrical campsites, seasonal campsites, as well as yurts along the lakeshore. Over 150 cottages are also located within the park. An angler's paradise, the lake is well-known as a place to catch lake trout and walleye.

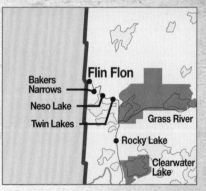

Bakers Narrows Provincial Park is located on both sides of Highway 10 about 27 kilometres southeast of Flin Flon. Nearby parks include Neso Lake, Twin Lakes, and Grass River. ■

Beaudry

THE ASSINIBOINE RIVER BETWEEN PORTAGE LA PRAIRIE and Winnipeg meanders its way through relatively flat land, sometimes even looping back on itself. On a map, the path of the river appears to be almost randomly doodled by a creative cartographer. Beaudry Provincial Park just west of Headingley straddles the Assiniboine at one of these curvaceous points. It became a provincial park in 1974.

With a variety of trees and ground cover, Beaudry is particularly lovely in the fall.

Historically, the land occupied by Beaudry was part of the area that was known as the White Horse Plains. Beaudry is also on the eastern edge of the old Metis settlement that was founded by Cuthbert Grant in 1824. Reverend Patrick Beaudry was the first Metis priest in the West.

Several walking trails pass through Beaudry's well-known mature floodplain forests of cottonwood, aspen, oak, elm, maple, and basswood. Some of the trees are huge and centuries old. In places, dense stands of ostrich ferns cover the ground, and in other places, climbing riverbank grapes scale some of the trees. With such a variety of trees and ground cover, Beaudry is particularly lovely in the fall. All of the walking trails, varying in length from two to five kilometres, are named after trees. In the winter, the trails become groomed cross-country ski trails. Many unnamed trails also wind through the forest. A sheltered kiosk near the parking lot provides park information and trail maps.

At 9.5 square kilometres in size, Beaudry may be relatively small in area, but big in landscape variety. In addition to its mature forests, Beaudry is also home to a restored tall grass prairie with big bluestem, porcupine grass and other prairie plants. In the late 1980s, seeds were collected from nearby prairie rem-

nants and sown at Beaudry. Take in this effort to bring back a bit of the pre-settlement landscape by wandering around and across the natural prairie on a walking path. The park's area south of Provincial Road 241 is home to a wetland, with marsh vegetation and wildlife. To explore the Assiniboine River, the park has a canoe launch near the parking lot.

Beaudry is located about 10 kilometres west of Winnipeg on PR 241, also known as Roblin Boulevard. ■

Beaver Creek

From the shore of Beaver Creek, visitors can gaze across the bay at the Grindstone peninsula area of Hecla/Grindstone Provincial Park.

IN COMPARISON TO OTHER LAKE WINNIPEG PROVINCIAL PARKS, Beaver Creek seems far away. Of all eight Lake Winnipeg parks — Elk Island, Grand Beach, Patricia Beach, Winnipeg Beach, Camp Morton, Hnausa Beach, Hecla/ Grindstone, and Beaver Creek — Beaver Creek boasts the most northerly Lake Winnipeg campground. That said, it is only a 2-hour drive north of Winnipeg; not far by most standards, but far enough to be away from the hustle and bustle of crowds and traffic. If you just want to relax and breathe, listen to the sound of the quiet, and maybe watch the stars, then Beaver Creek is for you.

Beaver Creek is located along the shore of Lake Winnipeg's Washow Bay. In the late 1940s after the Second World War, the provincial government began several land settlement projects, clearing and draining land, surveying, and constructing roads. By that time, prime agricultural land had been long settled, and the land settlement projects were located in agricultural fringe areas on land less suited for agriculture. One of the projects was located north of Riverton along Washow Bay, south of Beaver Creek.

By the mid-1950s the demand for summer home lots remained high, and it was becoming increasingly difficult to find suitable lakeshore property for subdivision, particularly in the southern part of the province. The province made lots available at Beaver Creek, and by 1957, a campground, picnic area, and beach were also developed.

Beaver Creek was designated a provincial park in 1961. Today, the park has a campground with 15 basic campsites, picnic areas, a boat launch, and a small beach. The park also accommodates more than 50 cottages located both north and south of the campground area. From the park, visitors can gaze across the bay to the Grindstone peninsula area of Hecla/ Grindstone Provincial Park.

Beaver Creek is located about 40 kilometres north of Riverton. Follow Highway 8 north until its intersection with Provincial Road 234, then continue on PR 234. ■

Bell Lake

THE PORCUPINE HILLS, A RANGE OF HILLS somewhat circular in appearance on a map and the northern-most part of the Manitoba Escarpment, is one of the highest areas of elevation within the province. While Baldy Mountain at 831.2 metres above sea level in Duck Mountain Provincial Park gets the nod for the highest point in Manitoba, Hart Mountain in the Porcupine Hills at 823 metres above sea level is not far behind. The area just north of the community of Swan River is well-known for its forests and clear lakes. The Porcupine Provincial Forest, formerly the Porcupine Forest Reserve first created in 1906, covers much of the area.

(left) For rock hounds, Bell Lake's rocky shoreline is a geological treat.

In addition to logging, the Porcupine Hills area has always been popular with big game hunters. A 1913 big game report noted that "the Porcupine Hills are the browsing ground of great quantities of moose that are reported to be bigger, darker, and to carry better heads than any in Manitoba." The area is also home to deer, black bears, and many smaller mammals.

Interest in creating a summer resort at Bell Lake in the Porcupine Hills emerged back in the early 1930s. By 1932, a committee of residents from both Bowsman and Minitonas studied the possibility, and reported that only five miles of road would have to be cut from the Hart Mountain trail to the lake. It was not until 1955 that road construction began.

Bell Lake Provincial Park, designated in 1974, occupies a small 0.04 square kilometre area on the lake's shore. The park has eight basic campsites, a picnic area and a boat launch. For rock hounds, Bell Lake's rocky shoreline is a geological treat. For anglers, the lake is a popular spot for catching northern pike and walleye. The park also serves as a staging point for hunters in the fall.

Bell Lake is one of three provincial parks in the Porcupine Provincial Forest — see also North Steeprock and Whitefish Lake. Bell Lake is on Provincial Road 365 about 17 kilometres from Highway 10, just north of Birch River. ◼

Bell Lake

Birch Island

BIRCH ISLAND PROVINCIAL PARK, designated in 2010, takes its name from Birch Island, the largest island in Lake Winnipegosis. As Manitoba's second largest lake after Lake Winnipeg, Lake Winnipegosis covers 5,370 square kilometres in total and is approximately 200 kilometres long with a maximum width of about 35 kilometres. It has a mean depth of 4.2 metres, making it a shallow lake for its size. The lake is dotted with numerous islands and reefs. Birch Island Provincial Park encompasses about 790 square kilometres in the heart of Lake Winnipegosis, including Birch Island, many smaller islands and reefs, and open water.

Famous for its diversity of colonial water bird species, Lake Winnipegosis is home to the largest breeding population of cormorants in the province. Although most cormorants nest on the ground, some nest in trees. In addition to double-crested cormorants, the lake is home to American white pelicans, gulls (herring, California, and ring-billed), terns (common, Caspian, and Forster), and herons (great blue and black-crowned night).

Lake Winnipegosis is also an important commercial fishing lake that produced well over a million kilograms of fish in each of the last several years. In the past, cormorant eggs, nestlings, and adult birds were destroyed due to the belief that the birds reduced catches of commercially valuable fish. Studies indicate, though, that cormorants feed primarily on fish that have little commercial value, mainly yellow perch, white suckers and tullibee, while pelicans favour sticklebacks,

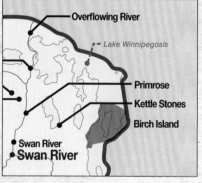

followed by suckers. Cormorants and pelicans are protected species under the provincial *Wildlife Act*, and gulls, terns and herons are protected under the federal *Migratory Birds Convention Act*. The designation of Birch Island as a provincial park is a further level of protection to help maintain the birds' nesting habitat.

Birch Island Provincial Park is not road accessible and there are no facilities within the park. If accessing the park by water is of interest, the closest community to the park is Duck Bay, north of Camperville. ∎

Lake Winnipegosis is home to the largest population of breeding cormorants in the province.

Birch Island

Dennis Fast

Birch Point

TO MANY PEOPLE, BEAUTIFUL LAKE OF THE WOODS epitomizes the Canadian Shield recreation experience, and many Manitobans travel into Ontario to access the vast lake. Extensive black spruce and tamarack bog areas generally limit access to the portion of Lake of the Woods that reaches into southeast Manitoba. But Birch Point, a narrow spit formation on Buffalo Bay, is strategically located on the edge of the vast bog. A road to Birch Point from Moose Lake provides a local option for accessing Lake of the Woods. Visitors can also access Lake of the Woods farther south in Buffalo Point First Nation. In the eighteenth and nineteenth centuries, the lake was on the fur trade route between Lake Superior and Lake Winnipeg.

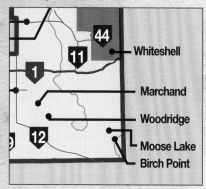

Lake of the Woods is divided into two very different areas. The northern, irregularly-shaped part in northwestern Ontario is deep with rocky shores and numerous islands, while the southern part, much more rounded in appearance on a map, is essentially an open shallow body of water. From the shore of Birch Point on Buffalo Bay, Lake of the Woods appears endless with its far shore nowhere in sight.

Birch Point and Moose Lake are situated within the Northwest Angle Provincial Forest, established as a forest reserve in 1956 in the extreme southeast corner of the province. First developed in 1960 and designated a provincial park in 1961, Birch Point is a small 0.13 square kilometre park with a small sandy beach, a campground with 26 basic campsites, a picnic area and boat launch. Many visitors stay at the larger campground or lodge at neighbouring Moose Lake Provincial Park. As with Moose Lake, Birch Point is popular with locals but also with Americans due to its proximity to the United States.

The easiest way to get to Birch Point is via Highway 12 to Sprague, then Provincial Road 308 from Sprague to Moose Lake. To get to Birch Point, visitors must travel through Moose Lake Provincial Park and follow PR 509 from the southwest corner of Moose Lake near the campground, south to Birch Point — a short six-kilometre drive. ■

Birch Point

Birds Hill

THE SUPER-SIZED "FREQUENT DEER CROSSINGS NEXT 10 KM" sign on Highway 59 near Birds Hill Park says it all. Just northeast of Winnipeg, Birds Hill is one of Manitoba's most visited provincial parks, popular with both people and deer. Established in 1964 and officially opened in 1967 to celebrate Canada's centennial, Birds Hill is utilitarian and all-season, catering to many activities of the nearby urban population. Camping, swimming, running, cycling, roller-blading, walking, horseback riding, cross-country skiing, snowmobiling — all, and more, are possible within the 35 square kilometres of the park.

Birds Hill sits atop a large gravel deposit, eskers deposited by glacial melt water thousands of years ago. Named for Curtis Bird, doctor and member of the Manitoba Legislature, and his father James Bird, Hudson Bay Company factor who owned a large tract of land in the area, the hill provided safety for settlers who sought its modest elevation during the great Red River floods of 1826 and 1852. A look-out tower is on Griffiths Hill, the highest point in the park with an elevation of 265 metres above sea level. In comparison, downtown Winnipeg is 232 metres above sea level. On a clear day, the most recognizable sight from the

Birds Hill sits atop a large gravel deposit, eskers created by glacial melt water thousands of years ago.

tower is, in fact, downtown Winnipeg, just over 20 kilometres away.

European settlers arrived in the area in the late nineteenth century, some farming the land until the park was created in their midst. Although the park feels like it has always been a recreational destination, in fact, over 150 private properties in the rural municipalities of Springfield and St. Clements were expropriated in the mid-1960s to establish the park. The Kudlowich homestead remains a point of interest along the Pine Ridge trail, named for the former community of Pine Ridge that once occupied land in the vicinity of the park. An old kiln along the Lime Kiln trail was used to make quicklime by burning limestone gravel for the purposes of making whitewash, plaster and mortar. Pine Ridge cemetery reminds us of the park's settlement history.

In *The Fragile Lights of Earth* published in 1978, Gabrielle Roy reminisced, "When I was young in

Birds Hill

Manitoba, one of our favourite outings was a trip to Birds Hill. What was so attractive about it then? From the level plain there arose, for no apparent reason, a singular, long, sandy crest, the shore, one would have said, of some ancient lake, dry for centuries and turned to land, grass and market gardens, except in certain parts where brush allowed the persistence of wild life, and where one heard the plaintive cry of birds."

Although no one lives in Birds Hill Provincial Park today, the campground with over 400 basic, electrical, and full service campsites is a popular temporary summer haven for locals and visitors alike. Group use campsites are also available by reservation for large groups.

Included within the park, and adjacent to the campground, is a man-made lake. For the 1999 Pan Am Games, the lake was divided into two, separating the popular recreational beach and swimming portion

from Kingfisher Lake. Stocked with trout, Kingfisher Lake has a wheelchair accessible fishing pier. Groundwater is pumped into the swimming portion of the lake to help ensure that it meets recreational water quality guidelines. Walk, cycle, blade or skateboard the seven-kilometre paved trail that surrounds the man-made lake. With its dips, curves, and lovely views, it is sure to please.

If horse activities are of interest, the Manitoba Horse Council's Equestrian Centre near the riding stable is often a site for polo, dressage, jumping and driving. Shortly after opening, the park hosted the 1967 Pan Am Games equestrian events. Trail rides, hay rides in the summer, and sleigh rides in the winter are popular activities for both kids and adults. Many horse owners live just outside the park and several horse trails through the park cater to this crowd.

Within the relatively small confines of Birds Hill's boundaries, several types of plant communities

The Kudlowich homestead remains a point of interest along the Pine Ridge trail, named for the former community of Pine Ridge that once occupied land in the vicinity of the park.

can be explored. In the early days of park creation, several thousand trees were planted to help transition the park from agricultural grassland. Walk the one kilometre Bur Oak trail, paved to accommodate wheelchair use, and visit a forest of gnarled bur oak trees. Or for something completely different, take the 3.5 kilometre Cedar Bog trail to experience a cool, damp, shady bog populated with eastern white cedars. If wildflowers are of interest, watch for the south drive meadow carpeted with three-flowered avens, commonly known as prairie smoke, or yellow lady's slippers along road allowances. Whatever the vegetation, the sighting of white-tailed deer is common, and always remains a pleasure. When the sun goes down and the wind calms, listen for the howls of coyotes and wolves for a reminder that there is still a bit of wilderness in the park, if only a little bit. Also listen for birdsong — more than 200 bird species have been identified in Birds Hill by the keen eyes of birders.

And birdsong is not the only sound worth seeking. Music, man. Every July, the park swells with approximately 50,000 music-lovers attending the Winnipeg Folk Festival. First staged in 1974 to celebrate Winnipeg's centennial, the annual festival has continued to grow, attracting musicians and their fans from around the world. ■

Burge Lake

BURGE LAKE IS ONE OF TWO PROVINCIAL PARKS situated near the town of Lynn Lake, and like many other Canadian Shield parks, its establishment was closely linked to the development of the local mining industry. Lynn Lake was established in the late 1940s as Manitoba's first nickel mining community. With the decline of mining near Sherridon located to the south, buildings were lifted off their foundations and moved to Lynn Lake. During the winters of 1952 and 1953, 13 homes, two churches, three stores, a bank and a school annex were sledded over 250 kilometres on a winter trail by tractor train. With the arrival of the Canadian National Railway in 1953, the building boom began, accompanied by the desire for recreation.

Although Lynn Lake's mining boom has, for the present, passed, the town bills itself as the Sportfishing Capital of Manitoba due to its proximity to many clean, clear northern lakes. Northern Manitoba is of course chock full of lakes, and Provincial Road 391 from Thompson to Lynn Lake, officially opened in 1974, makes the lakes around the town of Lynn Lake road-accessible — something not many northern lakes can boast.

Burge Lake Provincial Park, located about 10 kilometres from Lynn Lake, is accessible from PR 398. The park sign still says "Berge Lake",

The beach at Burge Lake is a popular northern swimming spot in the summer.

but according to the Manitoba Geographical Names Program, the lake is named after Glyguaid R. Burge, president of Giant Yellowknife Gold Mines, who had been a Royal Navy pilot during the Second World War before coming to Canada. Established as a provincial park in 1961, the park was used by residents of Lynn Lake in the decade prior to its official designation. It has an area of 0.06 square kilometres.

Like its nearby sister park, Zed Lake, Burge Lake is set in the sandy soils of the Churchill River upland portion of the Canadian Shield. The park includes a small campground with eight basic sites. The campground is located at 56.90 degrees north in latitude, making it the second most northerly provincial park campground, after Zed Lake. And because of its northerly latitude, anyone camping on or near June 21 would notice almost 18 hours of sunlight, plus over an hour of twilight in both morning and evening.

The beach at Burge Lake is larger than the beach at Zed Lake, making it a popular swimming spot in the summer. A boat launch provides access to the lake, an angling destination for lake trout, walleye and northern pike. The park also accommodates 24 cottages.

Burge Lake

Camp Morton

ESTABLISHED BY FATHER THOMAS MORTON and Archbishop A. A. Sinnott in 1920 after the First World War, Camp Morton was a fresh air camp for Roman Catholic children for decades until its closure in 1969. In 1972, the land was purchased by the province, and in 1974, Camp Morton and adjacent lands became a provincial park.

Many of the old buildings still stand, providing historical points of interest.

In its heyday, the camp hosted boys in July and girls in August, accommodating up to 300 children at any one time. Many of the old buildings, including the chapel, water tower, pump house, and several other stackwall buildings still stand, and provide historical points of interest. To construct the stackwall buildings, logs were layered horizontally as if stacked in a wood-pile, and held together by mortar. From the outside, an observer sees the round log ends in a wall of mortar, giving the walls a polka-dotted appearance. A recreation hall that was once used by children attending camp is still in use today. Old stone fences are also evident throughout the park, sometimes appearing in the most unusual places. Park the car near the campground office and walk across the open field to the far west side of the park. A path leads to Mary Knoll (knoll, as in "hill") with a sundial and formal gardens.

Over the years, Camp Morton Provincial Park has been well known for its family vacation cabins set in the typical mixed forest of the Interlake. The park also offers yurts, strategically placed along the Lake Winnipeg shoreline, for those visitors

who enjoy drifting off to sleep listening to the sound of the waves.

The entire park consists of several parcels of land, each with separate entrances accessible from Provincial Road 222 (an extension of Highway 9) just north of Gimli. Entrances at the south end provide access to a small campground with 19 basic campsites and an area with walking and cross country ski trails. The main area of the park contains the historical buildings, along with group use camping sites, cabins and yurts, a small beach, and the park's office. Camp Morton is one of eight provincial parks along the shores of Lake Winnipeg. See also Elk Island, Grand Beach, Patricia Beach, Winnipeg Beach, Hnausa Beach, Hecla/Grindstone, and Beaver Creek. ■

Caribou River

CARIBOU RIVER, AT 7,460 SQUARE KILOMETRES IN SIZE, is Manitoba's second largest provincial park after Sand Lakes, and along with Nueltin Lake, the most northerly. A wilderness park nestled in northeast Manitoba against the Nunavut border, Caribou River, which became a provincial park in 1994, is set in the transition area between boreal forest and tundra. The area is sometimes referred to as the barren lands and is also called by Aboriginals "land of little sticks" as tree growth is limited and stunted in this area of widespread permafrost where the subsoil remains frozen during the area's short summers.

Geologically, Caribou River is part of the northern Manitoba landscape where eskers and ancient beach ridges are prevalent. Eskers were formed as the last glacier melted, and sand and gravel carried in its drainage channels were deposited in elongated ridges on the surface of the ground. Over 740 esker segments have been mapped to date in northern Manitoba. The beach ridges were formed as the Tyrrell Sea receded to present day Hudson Bay. The park is home to Round Sand Lake, a lake almost completely ringed with sandy beaches.

As the name suggests, the Caribou River area is home to barren ground caribou, the most numerous caribou subspecies in Canada. Compared to other caribou subspecies, barren ground caribou have the biggest antlers. The caribou's habitat extends in a large area covering parts of northern Manitoba, northern Saskatchewan, Nunavut, and the

Northwest Territories. Caribou use the area's eskers and beach ridges as travel corridors.

In the 1930s, the Hudson's Bay Company erected a trading post at Caribou Lake that operated for only a few years. Part of the Sayisi Dene's traditional territory, one of the post's buildings is used as a shelter while hunting in the winter.

Hap Wilson and Stephanie Aykroyd declared the area alluring and addictive in *Wilderness Manitoba: Land Where the Spirit Lives*, published in 1999. "As one moves

Manitoba Conservation, Parks and Natural Areas Branch

Caribou River

Barren ground caribou use the area's eskers and beach ridges as travel corridors.

northeast away from the warmth and security of the boreal reaches, the land opens up and lays bare its soul," they noted, before lyrically adding, "here, human bones mingle congenially with those of caribou. This sub-arctic, heath-rich tundra has recorded the history and movements of animals and an ancient people for centuries, in a mosaic of pathways, gravestones, sun-bleached bones, way markers and abandoned campgrounds — stories of survival, of death, and of replenishment."

Caribou River Provincial Park is not road-accessible. Access for fly-in fishing and canoeing can be arranged with lodges, outfitters, or air charter companies. ■

Clearwater Lake

WHEN PEERING DOWN INTO THE CRYSTAL CLEAR WATER of Clearwater Lake, it is hard to determine if the depth is one metre, or several. Clearwater Lake, the star attraction of Clearwater Lake Provincial Park, is a lake of exceptional clarity with high quality surface water.

Considered one the best road-accessible trout fishing lakes in Manitoba, the lake also provides a source of genetic stock for Manitoba's lake trout and whitefish stocking programs. Lake trout and whitefish egg harvesting began in 1956. Unlike most other fish species that spawn in spring, lake trout spawn in the fall. They take about eight years to fully mature. To protect lake trout spawning, Clearwater Lake is partially closed in the fall to angling and restrictions on catch limits are in place. Of course, trout is not the only fish species in the lake. In the spring, northern pike and white suckers navigate a fishway in Jackfish Creek to spawn in Campbell Lake, a small lake just south of Clearwater Lake.

Clearwater Lake was also once known as Atikameg Lake (Cree for whitefish). The lake was located in the southern part of the Cormorant Forest Reserve, designated in 1948. As soon as the forest reserve was created, recreational development

The Caves hiking trail leads to an excellent close-up view of dolomite cliffs.

began in earnest with fishing and hunting lodge permits, followed by cottage developments in 1949. Due to its proximity to The Pas, some cottages along the lakeshore had also been constructed in the decades prior to forest reserve status. Even today, the park's 365 cottages include a mix of leased and privately owned lots. Clearwater Lake Provincial Park at 593 square kilometres in size was designated in 1962.

Development in the park is primarily confined to the park's southern edge. Campgrounds with 60 basic and electrical campsites, plus seasonal sites, are located at Campers Cove and Pioneer Bay, along with beaches at each location. Yurts are available at Campers Cove. Sunset Beach also has a picnic area. There are also privately run lodges located within the park. Adjacent to the park's southern boundary is The Pas

airport — a reminder of the park's close proximity to The Pas.

The one-kilometre long Caves hiking trail is accessible just west of Pioneer Bay. The trail leads to an excellent close-up view of dolomite cliffs — sedimentary rock deposited 400-500 million years ago. The "caves" are actually deep crevices that formed when rock separated from the cliffs. Broken and fallen rocks create a cave-like appearance in some places. The designated trail has stairways and viewing platforms for safety reasons, but there are many opportunities (and edges) to take a closer look. Parents watch your children! The trail also offers spectacular views of the true blue waters of Clearwater Lake.

To get to Clearwater Lake, take Highway 10 north of The Pas to Provincial Road 287. ∎

Colvin Lake

STANDS OF BLACK SPRUCE APPEARING STICK-LIKE and stunted grow in northern Manitoba's thin soils along with dwarf birch, Labrador tea, other low-growing shrubs, lichens, and mosses. Permafrost and short summers make the area inhospitable to significant tree growth. This "land of little sticks" covers an area that represents the transition between the boreal forest and the tundra.

Besides its stick-like stands of trees, the land itself is unusual in its appearance. Many eskers wind across the northern landscape, sometimes rising 50 metres above the surrounding area. Eskers formed during glaciation when melt water channels or tunnels within glaciers became filled with sand and gravel. When the glacier melted, winding, linear ridges of sand and gravel were deposited on the land. Eskers are featured in the Colvin Lake landscape in the extreme northwest part of Manitoba. And for some contrast to the esker landscape, the southern part of the park near Secter Lake is home to pink granite outcrops.

As with neighbouring Nueltin Lake Provincial Park located just to the northeast, Colvin Lake Provincial Park is part of the winter territory for barren ground caribou that use the eskers as travel corridors. The area is also home to a variety of animals including moose, black bear, lynx, weasel and mink, and is breeding habitat for a number of migratory bird species. As part of the traditional territory of the Northlands Denesu-

line First Nation, hunting, trapping and fishing occurs in the area.

In 1972, Colvin Lake was named for Frederick J. Colvin of Carman, a World War II casualty who served with the Winnipeg Grenadiers. Colvin Lake Provincial Park was designated a wilderness park in 2010. Many lakes in its 1631 square kilometre area drain into the Thlewiaza River, which flows through Nueltin Lake Provincial Park before exiting into Nunavut.

Colvin Lake Provincial Park is not road-accessible. Access for fly-in fishing and canoeing can be arranged with lodges, outfitters, or air charter companies. ■

For some contrast to the esker landscape, the southern part of the park is home to pink granite outcrops.

Colvin Lake

Criddle/Vane Homestead

SHORTLY AFTER MANITOBA BECAME A PROVINCE in 1870, promotional literature billing the prairies as the land of immeasurable promise and the healthiest climate of the world was distributed to attract settlers. Europeans responded, including Londoner Percy Criddle. Percy, though, was not a farmer — he was a merchant with a variety of academic interests. In an unusual ménage à trois, he also fathered children with both his wife Alice and his mistress Elise.

In August 1882 Percy, Alice, Elise, and their nine children arrived in southwestern Manitoba, homesteading in the rolling countryside southeast of Brandon near the community of Treesbank. Unskilled in farming, the family spent much of the difficult early years focussed on mere survival. The Criddle and Vane homestead eventually became quite different than other pioneer homesteads. As sports fans, their acreage included a cricket pitch, golf course, and an area for tennis. With interest in the arts and sciences, their home included a library, billiard table, organ, and telescope. And as avid naturalists, the family was interested in the wildlife and plants that surrounded them, and in sharing that knowledge with others.

Not long after their arrival in Canada, Percy became a volunteer weather observer for the Meteorological Service of Canada under the station name St. Albans. Until recently, lightning rods stood tall on the roof of the Criddle home. Son Norman was a well-known biologist and was appointed Entomologist for Manitoba. His entomology laboratory, a short distance from the house, still stands. The other point of interest on the property is the family

cemetery with heart-shaped headstones marking the graves of Percy and Alice. If reading more about this eccentric family interests you, in 1973, Percy's granddaughter Alma Criddle published a history of the Criddles called *Criddle-de-Diddle-Ensis* that includes excerpts from Percy's diaries.

The Manitoba government acquired the 1.32 square kilometre property in the 1970s and the Criddle/Vane Homestead became a provincial heritage park in 2004. Wander the homestead's lovely woods and meadows while appreciating these eccentric pioneer families who found a unique kind of success on the Canadian prairies.

Criddle/Vane Homestead is about three kilometres east of Provincial Road 340 just south of Shilo. ∎

Duck Mountain

THE MANITOBA ESCARPMENT STRETCHES from the Pembina Hills in the south to the Porcupine Hills in the northwest. From below the escarpment, the Duck Mountains, also known as "the Ducks", appear as an impenetrable, forest-covered rise. Forest-covered, yes, but fortunately, not impenetrable. Perched on the escarpment, Duck Mountain Provincial Park covering 1,424 square kilometres has a rolling landscape with numerous lakes and wetlands created when the last glacier melted about 10,000 to 12,000 years ago.

To many, Duck Mountain is an area known for its outstanding natural beauty. To others, the reputation of Duck Mountain Provincial Park has been affected by the existence of logging operations in the park. Duck Mountain is currently the only provincial park in which forestry is permitted. Forestry, though, has been an integral part of the area's history for over a century.

In the latter part of the nineteenth century, growth of agricultural settlement spread at the base of the Manitoba Escarpment and in the valleys separating the upland areas. By 1899, the Canadian Northern Railway reached Swan River. Settlers needed timber for their homesteads, and in turn supplied labour for the forest industry in winter. Mills were located both south and north of the Ducks in Grandview and Swan River. The Duck Mountain Forest Reserve was established in 1906.

Forest fires in Duck Mountain used to be a continual threat. Descriptively named due to the absence of trees at its top, Baldy Mountain at 831 metres above sea level is Manitoba's highest point, and as the highest point and bald to boot, it made an ideal location for a forest fire lookout tower. The first tower was constructed at Baldy Mountain in 1914. Other towers were constructed in 1926 and 1957. As the surrounding forest grew taller after widespread forest fires in the late nineteenth century, Baldy Mountain lookout towers got taller to provide unobstructed views — while the first tower was 40 feet tall, the third tower was 80 feet tall. Cabins were also built to provide accommodation when the lookout towers were being used. A cabin at Baldy Mountain, built in 1925, can still be seen

Duck Mountain

Duck Mountain is an area known for its outstanding natural beauty.

today along the 3.5-kilometre Baldy Mountain trail. A central cache of fire-fighting equipment was established in the forest reserve at Cache Lake, just northeast of the Blue Lakes, and trails to the cache soon followed. Many of the trails were later used by forestry operations.

In 1930 the responsibility for natural resources was transferred from the federal government to the province. In its very first annual report, the department of Mines and Natural Resources noted that there was increasing use by campers in Duck Mountain, particularly near Singoosh and Blue Wing Lakes. By 1936, kitchenettes were constructed for campers. Access to the lakes was made possible by a road from the community of Ethelbert, east of the forest reserve. By 1943, Singush was stocked with trout and East Blue Lake was stocked with walleye to

Duck Mountain

attract anglers, and stocking of other lakes continued in subsequent years. In 1949, a road to Wellman Lake was completed, and Central Road construction from Grandview north began. In 1952, construction of an access road from the west began. In 1950, the first provincial summer home permits were issued for Duck Mountain. Duck Mountain Provincial Park was designated in 1961.

Today, Duck Mountain has four campgrounds with 275 basic, electrical, and electrical/water campsites, plus seasonal sites, at Blue Lakes, Childs Lake, Singush Lake and Wellman Lake. Privately operated lodges and resorts are also located within the park.

If you enjoy seeing the sights on foot, Duck Mountain has many options when it comes to walking trails. Copernicus Hill, so named in 1973 to commemorate the 500th anniversary of the birth of Polish astronomer Nicolaus Copernicus (who theororized that the earth and other planets revolved around the sun) is located near Glad Lake just south of Wellman Lake, and is known locally as Glad Hill. A 1.5 kilometre hike on the Copernicus Hill Hiking trail takes visitors to a viewing tower.

By the early 1930s, areas near Singoosh and Blue Wing Lakes were increasingly used by campers.

The 1.1-kilometre Shining Stone trail takes visitors from Blue Lakes campground around a peninsula that stretches into West Blue Lake. The lake reaches a depth of 37 metres. With no inlet or outlet, the lake is spring-fed from the lake's bottom. Alternatively, visitors can walk the more challenging 5.5-kilometre Blue Lakes Hiking trail, also accessible near Blue Lakes Campground.

Trails are also located at Childs Lake, Glad Lake, Shell River Valley, Spray Lake, and Mossberry Lake. Or walk through elk habitat on the Wapiti trail, just south of the junction of Provincial Roads 366 and 367.

In winter the park has cross-country ski trails and snowmobile trails.

If paddling is your preference, the park also has two fairly short designated canoe routes, including the 5.8-kilometre Chain Lakes Canoe Route north of Blue Lake, and the 6.4-kilometre Beaver Lake Canoe Route south of Glad Lake.

Access to Duck Mountain is either via Provincial Road 366, a north-south road between Grandview and Minitonas, or PR 367, an east-west road between Garland and San Clara. The two roads intersect near the middle of the park. ∎

Duck Mountain

Duff Roblin

CHARLES DUFFERIN ROBLIN WAS BORN INTO a political family in Winnipeg in 1917. His grandfather, Rodmond Roblin, had been Manitoba's Premier from 1900 to 1915. Duff was first elected to the Manitoba Legislature in 1949, and he served as Manitoba's Premier from 1958 to his resignation in 1967. Under his leadership, the province embarked on hydro development of the Nelson River, highways were built and upgraded, and investments were made in education, training, welfare, and medicine.

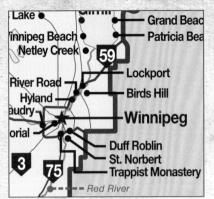

The map shows:
Lake, Grand Beac[h], Patricia Bea[ch], [W]innipeg Beach, Netley Creek, 59, Lockport, River Road, Birds Hill, Hyland, Winnipeg, [A]udry, [Mem]orial, 3, 75, Duff Roblin, St. Norbert, Trappist Monastery, Red River

After the 1950 Red River flood, a federal-provincial royal commission made recommendations for flood protection schemes. The commission recommended construction of the Red River Floodway, the Assiniboine/Portage Diversion and the Shellmouth Reservoir (see also Portage Spillway and Asessippi Provincial Parks). In 1962, Duff Roblin's government began construction of the Red River Floodway, affectionately known as "Duff's Ditch." The 47-kilometre long excavated channel begins just south of St. Norbert and ends at Lockport. Flow into the floodway is regulated by a control structure consisting of two gates

(left) The park commemorates the engineering feat of the Red River Floodway and the creation of a system of provincial parks.

located in the river just downstream of the floodway's inlet. Normally the gates are submerged and the Red River flows through the heart of Winnipeg. When flooding threatens, the gates are raised creating a partial dam in the river, raising the river's level south of the city and causing it to flow over the floodway's inlet structure. Used several times since its completion in 1968, expansion of the floodway's capacity began in 2005.

Duff Roblin's legacy also includes the establishment of a province-wide system of provincial parks. His government passed the first *Provincial Parks Act* in 1960, and in 1961, our first provincial parks were officially established.

Duff Roblin died in 2010. Duff Roblin Provincial Park, a heritage park, commemorates the engineering feat of the Red River Floodway and the creation of a system of provincial parks — both accomplishments much appreciated by Manitobans today. The original Duff Roblin park reserve was located just east of the intersection of Highway 59 and Winnipeg's north perimeter highway. In 2008, the park was moved to the Red River Floodway's inlet control structure. It is accessible from Highway 75 just south of Winnipeg. ∎

Duff Roblin

Elk Island

ELK ISLAND, 10.7 SQUARE KILOMETRES IN SIZE, is located at the north end of the Rural Municipality of Victoria Beach on the east side of Lake Winnipeg. Although most people associate Elk Island Provincial Park with the island itself, the park also includes the very tip of the mainland. A sand bar located just under the surface of the water keeps the island and mainland *almost* connected. On calm summer days, visitors often wade across to the island slowly feeling their way along the sand bar through water about waist high. During significant drought years, the sand bar is much more exposed making the distance between Elk Island and the mainland somewhat variable, and the depth more manageable for walkers. In the past visitors have walked across through water only inches deep.

Elk Island was on the fur trade route to and from the east that followed the Winnipeg River to Lake Winnipeg. It was named Isle du Biche (Deer Island) by fur trader and explorer Joseph La France and Isle aux Biches by La Verendrye. Other variations followed, including Isle of

Those who land on Elk Island's shore like to think of the island as a secret idyll.

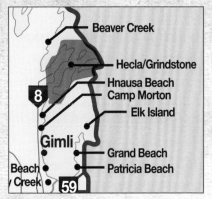

Beaver Creek

Hecla/Grindstone

Hnausa Beach
Camp Morton

8

Elk Island

Gimli

Beach
Creek

59

Grand Beach
Patricia Beach

Hinds, Stag Island, and Island of Elks. When the Victoria Beach Investment Company began acquiring land in 1911 for the purposes of resort development, Elk Island was included in their holdings. In the early twentieth century, Elk Island supported fishing stations, a mink ranch, and a group camp. A "veritable paradise of wild fruit", Elk Island was, and still is, popular with local berry pickers.

In 1970, the boundary of Grand Beach Provincial Park was extended to include Elk Island, and in 1974, the island became an independent provincial park. Elk Island is popular with beachcombers, hikers, canoeists, and kayakers. Those who land on Elk Island's shore like to think of the island as a secret idyll. Walk the island or lounge on almost deserted beaches — the ideal place to enjoy solitude while knowing that civilization is just over a kilometre away.

To get to Elk Island, take Highway 59 north to Victoria Beach and continue north on Provincial Road 504. The lake can be accessed right at the end of the highway. Parking is limited, so watch for signs that indicate where parking is allowed along the highway. ■

Elk Island

Grand Beach

GRAND BEACH MIGHT BE THE BEST BEACH IN MANITOBA, or certainly the most popular. What makes a beach the best? Three kilometres of amazingly fine white sand, a gentle gradient making for lots of room to play in shallow water, and dynamic 12-metre scenic sand dunes that back the beach. A kind of living landscape, the dunes can disappear in fierce Lake Winnipeg storms and regenerate months later. As one of the best beaches in Manitoba, it is probably the most well-attended when temperatures climb in summer and "at times you can't see the sand for the people". The beach has a dual personality with two beaches, east and west, separated by a channel that connects the lagoon to the lake. Depending on your mood or your preference, you can visit the busier see-and-be-seen west beach, or the more sedate east beach.

In the late 1700s the area was dubbed Grand Marais or "big marsh" by La Verendrye. In 1914, the Canadian Northern Railway acquired 150 acres of land to build a summer resort that would rival the CPR's Winnipeg Beach resort on the other side of the lake. By 1916, railway tracks had been laid and the first train arrived. The Grand Beach line even showed a profit in the Great Depression of the 1930s with Moonlight Special trains carrying beach-goers for bathing, dancing and fishing. The resort boasted the Grand Beach Hotel, a massive dance pavilion, boardwalk, and other amenities. The dance hall was destroyed by fire on Labour Day in 1950.

The development of Manitoba's highway network saw a corresponding decline in rail travel. The extension of Highway 59 north of Highway 44 in 1960 opened direct access to the beaches on the east side of Lake Winnipeg.

The province acquired the CNR property in 1961, and with some additional land, it became Grand Beach Provincial Park, one of Manitoba's first provincial parks. Despite its heyday as a railway resort, the park today appears relatively natural while the huge buildings of yesteryear live on only in interpretive signage. While most famous for its beach, the park is also home to a large campground with over 350 basic and electrical

campsites plus seasonal sites, over 500 cottages, and concessions.

Grand Beach Provincial Park is also home to several walking trails. The one-kilometre Spirit Rock trail traces the peninsula at the western-most end of the beach, while the one-kilometre Wild Wings trail traces a peninsula that extends into the large lagoon. Walk the 2.1-kilometre Ancient Beach trail with its trailhead near the campground to visit Lake Agassiz beach ridges. The sand ridge is part of the Belair moraine deposited by glaciers over 14,000 years ago. The highest part of the moraine is 40 metres higher than Lake Winnipeg, making for a spectacular view of the lake from the top of the trail. The Ancient Beach trail intersects with a number of other hiking and biking trails on the ridge that are also excellent cross-country ski trails in the winter.

Although birders can see about 100 different bird species in the park, one of the most notable species is the piping plover. Because piping plovers love the same wide open stretches of

beach as the rest of us do, piping plover populations have been in decline. Piping plover nests on Grand Beach are usually protected by both fences and a piping plover guardian who can answer any questions you might have about the birds.

To get to Grand Beach, take Highway 59 north of Winnipeg to Highway 12. Grand Beach is one of eight provincial parks along the shores of Lake Winnipeg. See also Elk Island, Patricia Beach, Winnipeg Beach, Camp Morton, Hnausa Beach, Hecla/Grindstone, and Beaver Creek. ∎

Grand Rapids

DURING THE FUR TRADE, GRAND RAPIDS on the Saskatchewan River marked the entrance to the major transportation route to the northwest. Over the last seven kilometres of its journey, the Saskatchewan River dropped 21 metres before entering Lake Winnipeg. While paddlers could ride the rapids heading toward the lake, a trip west meant a long portage for at least two kilometres past the most tumultuous part of the rapids. In 1877, a tramway was constructed to haul goods along the old portage route just north of the river. For several thousand years, Grand Rapids was also the site of a thriving sturgeon fishery.

Park use changes over time, and Grand Rapids is an example of a park in transition.

When construction of the Grand Rapids Generating Station got underway, an influx of fishermen and visitors strained available accommodations. A government campground was established on the south bank of the Saskatchewan River in view of the rapids, and for a while it was extremely popular. Completion of the generating station in 1963, however, stilled the rapids and altered the course of the river, leaving the campground along a mostly dry river bed without the sound of rushing water.

The campground with 30 basic campsites was maintained for a number of years after dam construction.

It became Grand Rapids Provincial Park in 1974. But the park and its campground received little traffic, probably because of its distance from Highway 6, and its distance from water. The campground has since fallen out of use and only vague reminders of its recreational past remain. Set in mature, tall forest, the campsite clearings are in the process of re-vegetating. There are no amenities in the park for visitors. Park use changes over time, and Grand Rapids is an example of a park in transition.

Grand Rapids Provincial Park is one park that is easy to miss. There is no signage pointing to the park, although it is road accessible albeit via an uneven gravel road off Highway 6 south of the community of Grand Rapids. Stop and ask for directions and you just may elicit confused and uncertain looks. If you do ask for directions, many people still refer to the park as the "old government campground." ■

Grand Rapids

Grand Valley

THE ASSINIBOINE RIVER VALLEY in western Manitoba is truly a large-scale river valley. Thousands of years ago, the Assiniboine River carried huge volumes of glacial melt water, depositing sand and gravel in the river's delta just east of Brandon before emptying into Lake Agassiz (see Spruce Woods Provincial Park). Grand Valley Provincial Park, 0.26 square kilometres in size, sits on the side of the valley immediately adjacent to the Trans-Canada Highway about 13 kilometres west of Brandon at the junction of the Trans-Canada and Highway 459 (Highway 1A).

Grand Valley was initially purchased from landowner Frank Stott in 1959 for the purpose of creating a campground and picnic site under the Trans-Canada Highway Camp and Picnic Sites Agreement, an agreement that saw the establishment of several wayside parks for travellers. Grand Valley became a provincial park in 1961. Today, the park and campground are leased to a private operator.

In the years prior to selling a portion of his land to the province,

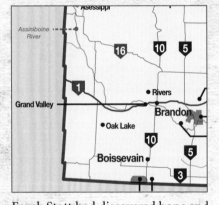

Frank Stott had discovered bone and other cultural artifacts on the surface of his land. Various archaeological excavations began in the 1940s. A plaque in the park commemorates the "Stott site". The Stott site itself is about 100 acres in size bisected by the Trans-Canada Highway, with Grand Valley Provincial Park on one side, and the remainder of the site on the other side of the highway.

Walk the Trail of the Buffalo Chase and make the sound of Trans-Canada Highway traffic disappear, at least for a little bit.

For a period of about 1,200 years, between 700 to 1,900 years ago, the Stott Site was a buffalo impoundment and village. The impoundment was constructed on the flood plain at the bottom of the valley wall, hiding it from the view of approaching bison until they were stampeded over the edge of the valley into the pound. Interpretive signs along the 1.5-kilometre Trail of the Buffalo Chase describe the entire bison hunt process, from runners finding herds, to driving and luring the bison toward the impoundment, to the kill and ceremonies surrounding the hunt. Walk the trail, and discover a fascinating history that will make the sound of Trans-Canada Highway traffic disappear, at least for a little bit. ∎

Grass River

WILD AND FREE, THE GRASS RIVER corridor has changed little since the days it was used during the fur trade in the eighteenth and nineteenth centuries. In the days when travelling the province's rivers provided access to the interior from York Factory on Hudson Bay, three routes were commonly used. The Grass River was part of the upper track that led to Cumberland House, the middle track included the Nelson River and also led to Cumberland House, and the lower track included the Hayes River that led south to Norway House and Lake Winnipeg. Hudson Bay Company men Joseph Smith (1763) and Samuel Hearne (1774, 1775, and 1776) were believed to be the first explorers and fur traders to paddle the Grass River. By the 1790s, fur trading posts were established on Reed Lake. Explorer and map-maker David Thompson wintered at Reed Lake while on his expeditions.

Established in 1962, Grass River Provincial Park at 2,279 square kilometres in size remains largely undeveloped for recreational purposes, making it appealing to those anglers, canoeists, and campers who prefer their parks in a pristine state. Minimal development protects the habitat of a small population of woodland caribou that often calves on the many

Visitors with an eye on the landscape will appreciate the park as a place where the Precambrian Shield meets the Manitoba Lowlands.

islands throughout the park and dines on lichens, sedges and shrubs.

Visitors with an eye on the landscape will appreciate the park as a place where the Precambrian Shield meets the Manitoba Lowlands, and granite meets limestone. Walk the 3.2-kilometre Karst Springs trail, the only designated trail in the park accessible from Iskwasum Campground, to learn more about these geological areas. The mossy and lush lower part of the trail leads to a burbling stream that empties into Iskwasum Lake. Further up the trail, the stream emerges from a limestone cliff. It has been speculated that the spring's source is Leak Lake located just south of the spring. Leak Lake was aptly named by T. Plunkett, a surveyor who believed that water leaked from the lake through a hole in the limestone at its bottom.

The park is also home to an ecological reserve — the highest level of protection in Manitoba intended to preserve unique plants, animals, geological features or natural landscapes. In Grass River, the Palsa Hazel Ecological Reserve protects a remnant permafrost feature. Palsas are

peat mounds 1.5 to six metres high and up to 100 metres in diameter with permanently frozen peat cores.

Highway 39, which connects Flin Flon and The Pas to Thompson, runs through the park's southern edge. Access to the park is primarily through three campground areas with over 120 basic campsites along Highway 39 — Reed Lake Campground on Reed Lake, Iskwasum Campground on Iskwasum Lake, and Gyles Campground on Simonhouse Lake. There are also privately-run lodges within the park. All of the lakes are popular with anglers seeking trophy catches of walleye, northern pike and trout. Simonhouse Lake also sports a good-sized natural beach.

The park is, of course, about the Grass River. To experience the river and its surroundings, trace the path of fur traders on the 725-kilometre Grass River Canoe Route that begins at First Cranberry Lake at the western edge of the park. Or if canoeing is not your preferred mode of transportation, drive Highway 39 (Highway 6 between Ponton and Thompson). Grass River Provincial Park is one of five provincial parks along the Grass River corridor, and is the farthest upstream. To see the river along its length, also visit Wekusko Falls, Sasagiu Rapids, Pisew Falls, and Paint Lake. ■

Hecla/Grindstone

ON MOONLIT NIGHTS, YOU MIGHT KEEP AN EYE OUT for Thorgeir's Boli (Thorgeir's Bull), a skinned bull calf dragging its bloodied hide and bellowing in the night. Legend has it that one of the first Icelandic settlers on Hecla Island was the great-granddaughter of an Icelandic sorcerer who who conjured up the bloody apparition during the 1700s. Thorgeir's Boli followed certain families for generations, and came to Canada with their descendants. It has allegedly been seen in various locations in New Iceland, including Hecla Island.

Hecla was home to a community of Icelanders for almost a century before it became a provincial park. First settled by Icelanders in 1876, Hecla was known to its residents as Mikley ("big island"). Initially part of New Iceland reserve, the area became part of Manitoba in 1881. At its population peak in the 1930s and '40s, about 500 people lived on Hecla.

Not long after Icelanders settled Hecla the summer "campers" arrived at Gull Harbour, first purchasing property along the harbour in 1896. By 1930, many cottages dotted the Gull Harbour shoreline. After ferry service began in 1953, a privately-operated lodge was developed to attract tourists. The northern tip of the island near Gull Harbour was designated a provincial recreation area in 1961. By the late 1960s, the permanent population of Hecla declined to less than 100. To reinvigorate the island and promote its tourism potential, a provincial park was proposed that would encompass the entire area. Hecla Provincial Park was officially designated in 1969.

The government began expropriating private land to make way for the park; a process that was not without controversy. Many saw irony in the government's intent to celebrate the island's Icelandic roots while displacing Heclingers who had called the island home for nearly a century. Gull Harbour cottagers were also expropriated. By the time the park was officially opened, a three-kilometre long causeway connecting the island to the mainland had been constructed, and a hotel and golf course were underway. The Hecla Historic Village area became a showcase heritage village without actual residents.

More than twenty years would pass before the government "re-settled" Hecla, offering cottage lots south of the Hecla Historic Village area and along the island's north shore. The lots were first offered to families of Hecla heritage. The Hecla Village cottage subdivision with about fifty five-acre cottage lots is the only provincial park cottage subdivision with landscape and architectural design guidelines to preserve and enhance the cultural character of the area.

In 1997, the park became known as Hecla/Grindstone Provincial Park. The "Grindstone" area of the mainland – a peninsula of land extending out into Lake Winnipeg — is also a popular cottaging area and had been designated a provincial recreation area in 1969. With a total area of 1,084 square kilometres, Hecla/Grindstone encompasses both land, including Black and Deer Islands, and adjacent waters. The park's eastern boundary stretches across to the east shore of Lake Winnipeg.

No Lake Winnipeg park is complete without beaches, and Hecla

Hecla/Grindstone

does not disappoint with Sunset Beach near the campground, and Gull Harbour Beach along the shores of Gull Harbour between the marina and the resort. Grindstone also has a public beach at Little Grindstone Point near the marina.

A variety of accommodations are available for visitors wanting to spend one night or several, including a campground with family vacation cabins, a bed and breakfast guesthouse, and a resort with a golf course. In 1912, the federal government established a fish hatchery on the island for both whitefish and pickerel.

The hatchery closed in 1936, but the building still exists and is currently a harbour-side restaurant.

With over 80 kilometres of trail for hiking or cycling, there are many options for getting out and about. The trails and boardwalks at Grassy Narrows Marsh near the causeway provide close-up views of the marsh and its inhabitants. The marsh trail system is comprised of several trails, from half a kilometre in length to almost 11 kilometres. Or try the scenic Lighthouse trail near the far end of the island, extending on a narrow stretch of land between Gull Harbour

For a leisurely and interesting walk, try the Hecla Village trail for a glimpse of Hecla's Icelandic past.

and the Lake Winnipeg narrows, and named, of course, for the lighthouse at the end of the trail. The Black Wolf trail, Hecla's newest walking trail, is a 25-kilometre trail that stretches between the Grassy Narrows Marsh and the group use camping area south of Hecla Village. Named for a small wolf pack that calls the island home, the trail includes signage that provides interpretive insight into wolf biology.

For a leisurely and interesting walk, try the one-kilometre Hecla Village trail for a glimpse of Hecla's Icelandic past. Visit six restored buildings, including a church, school, community hall, a traditional home, a boarding house, and the fish sta-

tion. And for a glimpse of history in print, read Doris Benson's novels, *A Place Called Hecla* and *When Home Can't Be Hecla* — highly readable fictionalized tales of Hecla residents mingled with a strong dose of Hecla's real heritage.

Just north of the village, view one of the most photographed and painted stretches of Hecla shoreline at the quarry picnic site where large layered fragments of sedimentary rock frame the spectacular view of lake and sky.

To get to Hecla Island, follow Highway 8 north of Winnipeg. Highway 8 ends at Gull Harbour. ∎

Hnausa Beach

EVERYBODY LOVES A BEACH, AND IF LOUNGING on a quiet piece of Lake Winnipeg shoreline appeals to you, then you will enjoy Hnausa (pronounced "Naysaw") Beach, located just south of the community of Hnausa about 34 kilometres north of Gimli.

In its early days, Hnausa was an Icelandic community in New Iceland, a reserve established in 1875 that stretched from Boundary Creek near Winnipeg Beach in the south to Hecla Island in the north. The area became part of Manitoba in 1881 and within a couple of decades, immigrants from other parts of Europe began arriving. Lake Winnipeg plays a central role in any community along its shores, and Hnausa is no exception. For early residents, fishing and winter freighting were common ways to make a living, augmented by agriculture and logging.

By 1906 the railway that had reached Winnipeg Beach in 1903 had stretched to Gimli, and in 1914, the first passenger train pulled into Hnausa on its way to Riverton. Over 400 people from towns along the railway rode the train in celebration. While the railway brought economic benefits as goods could be shipped to and from the area by train, it also opened the door for tourism. Land along the lake for recreation became a sought after commodity.

According to *Hnausa Reflections*, a local history published in 2004, the land now occupied by

Hnausa Beach Provincial Park was owned by Oddur Gudmundsson Akranes from 1887 to 1916. The land was divided, and a portion was purchased by Stefan Halldorson until he sold it in 1930 to the R.M of Bifrost. In 1930, the Bifrost Icelandic Committee requested that the R.M. of Bifrost contribute a portion of the land's purchase price, with the remainder to be paid by the committee. The R.M. of Bifrost became the property's official owner, and the land became a public park to be enjoyed by all. For many years, local Icelandic celebrations were held in the park. In 1959, the property was transferred to the province, and in 1961 Hnausa Beach became a provincial park.

Hnausa Beach has a campground with 45 basic and electrical campsites, a picnic area, a playground, and of course, a small sandy beach along the shore of Lake Winnipeg.

Hnausa Beach is located along Provincial Road 222 (an extension of Highway 9), about 34 kilometres north of Gimli. ∎

For many years, local Icelandic celebrations were held in the park.

Hnausa Beach

Hyland Park

IF PARKS COULD TALK, HYLAND PARK WOULD SURE-LY have some interesting tales to tell. Hyland Park is a small 0.05 square kilometre park just north of Winnipeg along the Red River in East St. Paul. Despite the unassuming appearance of the park, whose entrance is bordered by a gas station on one side and imposing hydro transmission lines on the other side, it has a colourful history. Named for the Hyland Navigation and Trading Company, the park was a music, dancing and picnicking destination for passengers on side-steamer Winnitoba and stern-steamer *Bonitoba* in the early part of the twentieth century. The steamers made several trips a day to the park, with music and dancing on every excursion.

In September 1912, only two years after its launch, the 57-metre long *Winnitoba* was destroyed by fire while docked at Hyland Park. Many speculated that the fire was deliberately set by picnickers seeking revenge on crewmen who had turned water hoses on them the day before to prevent them from overloading the boat. The *Bonitoba*, caught in the ice while docked at Hyland Park, suffered the river's icy wrath shortly thereafter. Low water levels in 1952 and 1987 exposed the wreck of the *Winnitoba*, enticing Winnipeggers

with a glimpse of their forgotten steamboat past.

The Lake Winnipeg Navigation Company's S.S. *Keenora* sailed daily to

Famous for its dance hall and picnic grounds, over 2000 people celebrated Canada's Jubilee in "Keenora" Park.

the park, and the park was known for a period of time as "Keenora Park". Still famous for its dance hall and picnic grounds, over 2,000 people celebrated Canada's Jubilee in Keenora Park in 1917. The dance hall, a wooden structure approximately 300 feet by 100 feet in size, was destroyed by fire in 1926.

Imperial Oil operated its refinery in East St. Paul beginning in the early 1950s, taking ownership of the land formerly known as Hyland and Keenora parks. When the company centralized its refining operations in Edmonton in the early 1970s, it donated the riverbank portion of its land to the province. In 1976, the province designated the land as a provincial recreation park.

Today, Hyland Park and adjacent land owned by Manitoba Hydro feature barbeque pits, a picnic shelter, tennis courts, public washrooms, and a boat launch. In 2006, the province leased Hyland Park to the R.M. of East St. Paul. ■

Kettle Stones

KETTLE STONES PROVINCIAL PARK, four square kilometres in size, is all about large and rather unique layered boulders, locally known as kettle stones. The park and its boulders have a heritage that goes back many millions of years. Scientists believe that kettle stones began to form between 70 to 135 million years ago when sediments were deposited on an ancient seabed, eventually becoming sandstone layers. Between one and 70 million years ago, uplift raised the sandstone layers above the level of the sea, and groundwater percolation combined with calcium carbonate from sea animal skeletons created "concretions" within the sandstone layer. About 8,500 years ago, wave action from Lake Agassiz eroded the softer sandstone, leaving behind the concretions, or kettle stones.

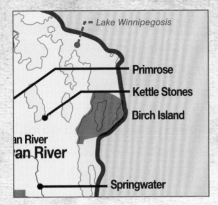

The only Manitoba location of kettle stones is within a small area on the north side of the Kettle Hills in the Swan-Pelican Provincial Forest, northeast of the community of Swan River and adjacent to the southeast shore of Swan Lake. The kettle stones, ranging in size from half a metre to 4.5 metres in diameter with heights generally between 2.5 and 3.5 metres, are concentrated in a small band about 300 metres wide and are randomly scattered over the landscape. They have a layered appearance

(left) Kettle stones have a layered appearance reflecting their sedimentary origins.

reflecting their sedimentary origins. Over the last several thousand years, weather has affected the appearance of the stones. Some have mosses and lichens growing on them, while others support tree growth. It is believed that many kettle stones still remain buried.

Kettle Stones became a provincial park in 1997. Although set in a provincial forest, the park is home to a mix of forest and prairie. Its meadows have patches of big bluestem, a grass usually associated with native tall grass prairie.

There is no road to Kettle Stones Provincial Park and condition of the access trail to the park is variable and often poor. Downed trees may occasionally block the trail. Travel by automobile is not recommended. All terrain vehicles and snowmobiles are commonly used to visit the park. Visitors to the Swan River Visitor Information Centre can view a kettle stone that was uncovered in 1966 during storm sewer excavations in the town of Swan River. ■

Lake St. Andrew

THE CENTRAL MANITOBA LOWLANDS, occupied by Manitoba's three largest lakes, is a visible legacy of glacial Lake Agassiz, which at one time covered the entire area. The region stretching between the lakes is generally a flat area with numerous small shallow lakes, marshes, fields, and forests mixed with aspen, birch, and a variety of conifers. The southern, mostly agricultural, part of the area gives way to more natural landscapes toward its central and northern portions.

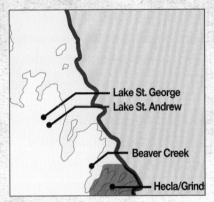

If fishing and hunting are of interest, then the "Saint Lakes" may hold great appeal. The Saint Lakes — Lakes St. Andrew, St. George, St. Patrick, St. David, and St. Michael — are located near Fisher Bay on Lake Winnipeg's west side, about a 2.5 hour drive north of Winnipeg. All the Saint Lakes are lakes with north-south orientations, etched into the landscape by ice erosion during glaciation. All are lakes named after patron saints of the British Isles, with Lake St. Andrew being named after the patron saint of Scotland. The Saint Lakes were commercially fished in the mid-twentieth century until

1963, and since that time, the lakes have remained popular for sport fishing and waterfowl hunting. Deer and moose hunting also occurs in the area.

Lake St. Andrew Provincial Park and its sister park, Lake St. George, both became provincial parks in 1974. Lake St. Andrew is a small roadside park at 0.02 square kilometres in size with a picnic area set in a grove of birch trees and a boat launch. Anglers may catch northern pike and perch, and the lake is occasionally stocked with walleye. While there are no campsites in the park, visitors can camp at Lake St. George, a few kilometres further north. There are also cottages along the lake outside of the park's boundaries.

Access to Lake St. Andrew Provincial Park and neighbouring Lake St. George Provincial Park is via Highways 7 and 17 to Hodgson, Provincial Road 224 to Dallas, then a gravel road known as Jackhead Road approximately 35 kilometres farther north to the parks. ■

The Saint Lakes are all named after patron saints of the British Isles, with Lake St. Andrew being named after the patron saint of Scotland.

Lake St. George

LAKE ST. GEORGE, NAMED FOR THE PATRON saint of England, is part of the Saint Lakes group located near Fisher Bay on Lake Winnipeg's west side. The Saint Lakes include Lakes St. George, St. Andrew, St. Patrick, St. David, and St. Michael. The area has long been popular for fishing and hunting. A tourist camp first began operating at Lake St. George in 1958. Despite its relative closeness to Winnipeg — about a 2.5 hour drive north — the area feels quite removed from any urban centre.

Lake St. George is fairly large with a surface area of 41 square kilometres, but it is shallow with a maximum depth of about three metres at its deepest points. It flows into Lake Winnipeg through the Jackhead River. Lake St. George Provincial Park, 0.21 square kilometres in size and officially designated in 1974, is located on the lake's eastern shore. It has a campground with 40 basic campsites, a picnic area, and a boat launch. For anglers, the lake has populations of northern pike, walleye

For anglers, the lake has populations of northern pike, walleye and perch.

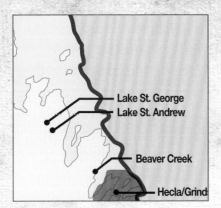

karst topography resulting from the last ice age. While a similar landscape near Narcisse a little farther south is home to garter snakes, at Lake St. George many of the caves are home to hibernating little brown bats. One of the caves supports thousands of little brown bats in the winter — the largest-known number of hibernating bats in the province. As the site is an ecological reserve, entry to the caves requires special permission.

and perch. There are also cottages on the lake, although not located in the park itself.

While not in the provincial park, the Lake St. George Ecological Reserve, just southeast of the lake, is a nearby natural treasure. The reserve contains many underground caves created by the movement of water through limestone — part of the

Access to Lake St. George Provincial Park and neighbouring Lake St. Andrew Provincial Park is via Highways 7 and 17 to Hodgson, Provincial Road 224 to Dallas, then a gravel road known as Jackhead Road approximately 35 kilometres farther north to the parks. ■

Lockport

S TAND IN THE MIDDLE OF LOCKPORT PROVINCIAL PARK, all 0.02 square kilometres of it, and take a look around. The St. Andrews Lock and Dam, completed in 1910 and now a national historic site, made river navigation over the St. Andrews rapids possible, and helps to maintain the river level upstream in Winnipeg. Anglers of all ages fish from shore and boats just downstream of the dam, catching walleye, sauger, and catfish. Even in winter, the site is a hub of angling activity as ice fishing huts dot the frozen river. Also looking for fish, huge flocks of pelicans visit in summer, sometimes bobbing on the water like floating white rafts. Watch the fish ladder at the northeast corner of the dam to see fish navigating the river, moving both upstream and downstream of the dam.

For all the visual distractions in the vicinity of the park, Lockport is a heritage park that commemorates the area's long history of Aboriginal use pieced together from numerous archaeological excavations over the last century and a half. Eight distinct layers, or strata, at the Lockport site have revealed artifacts and remains from four distinct cultures over a period of 3,000 years.

The Larter culture (1000 B.C. - 200 B.C.) represented the period of bison-hunting plains nomads. Plains hunters covered a huge territory to follow bison, occupying the Lockport site during the fall and winter when bison were at the northern edge of the plains, then following them south and west into the prairies with the coming of spring. The Laurel culture (200 B.C. - 1000 A.D.) represented a society that lived off rivers, lakes and forests. While this society hunted bison occasionally, other big game species like moose, caribou, deer and elk were more important. Smaller animals and birds were also hunted, and fish became a mainstay of the economy. During this culture, clay pottery was introduced in the region. The Blackduck and Selkirk cultures, similar late Woodland cultures, covered the period from 800 A.D. to 1700 A.D. By this period, corn agriculture was practised near Lockport until around 1500 A.D. when a colder

Lockport

For all the visual distractions in the vicinity of the park, Lockport is a heritage park that commemorates the area's long history of Aboriginal use.

and wetter climatic trend likely made the practice of growing corn unsuccessful.

Lockport became a provincial park in 1997. Interpretive signage around the park explains the site's rich Aboriginal history. The Kenosewun museum, also located in the park, suffered water damage and remains closed indefinitely.

Lockport Provincial Park is adjacent to Highway 44 and the Red River in the community of Lockport. ∎

Lundar Beach

THERE IS SOMETHING COMPELLING about the water in Lake Manitoba, the province's third largest lake, that makes you want to dive in or at least get your toes wet. Unlike Lake Winnipeg water that is slightly green and opaque in appearance, the water in Lake Manitoba is often pale turquoise with more clarity, especially when the weather is calm. Fortunately, if you want to indulge your desire for a refreshing dip there are five provincial "beach" parks along Lake Manitoba's shore — Lundar Beach, Manipogo, Margaret Bruce, St. Ambroise, and Watchorn.

Just south of Lundar Beach is a large Canada goose sanctuary.

Despite its relative proximity to Winnipeg, Lundar Beach is often quiet, except for its small but popular campground with over 30 basic and electrical campsites, plus seasonal sites. Extremely family-friendly, the park has a well-equipped day use area with a picnic shelter and playground. The sandy beach extends the entire length of the park, and beyond its borders in both directions. Perfect for a leisurely, and maybe barefoot, walk along its shore.

Similar to St. Ambroise Beach located a bit farther south, Lundar Beach is located along a beach ridge, with Lake Manitoba on one side and a marsh on the other side. Trails and boardwalks in the marsh maintained by volunteers lead to a viewing tower. Signage at trail entrances are hand-painted with songbirds, giving visitors a glimpse of what they might see on their walk. Also watch for ducks and pelicans. Pelicans and other water birds often roost on a rocky island offshore. Canada geese also migrate and breed in the area — just south of the park is Marshy Point Canada Goose Refuge and Wildlife Management Area.

The province began developing Lundar Beach as a recreational area in 1957. The area, 0.23 square kilometres in size, became a provincial park in 1961. The park also shares the shoreline with a cottage community.

To get to Lundar Beach Provincial Park, follow Highway 6 north to the community of Lundar, then follow Provincial Road 419 for about 18 kilometres to Lundar Beach; about 120 kilometres from Winnipeg. ∎

Lundar Beach

Manigotagan River

I F YOU HAVE VISITED OR PLAN TO VISIT Manigotagan
River Provincial Park, there is a good chance that you are a
whitewater paddler. For canoeists, the Manigotagan with its
numerous falls and navigable rapids has been a favourite for
years. The park, though, was just designated in 2004.

Manigotagan means "bad throat" in Cree. According to the Geographical Names Program, a chief camped at the mouth of the river heard a moose calling with "a peculiar sound in its throat." As a result, the river has, in the past, been called Bad Throat River.

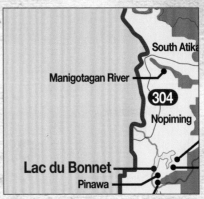

The 134-kilometre Manigotagan River begins in Ontario's Woodland Caribou Provincial Park and flows through eastern Manitoba's boreal forest into Lake Winnipeg. The park extends 45 kilometres along the river's length and reaches 750 metres from each riverbank, making it a long narrow park, 74.3 square kilometres in size. Home to a variety of large mammals including moose, caribou, and black bears, the park also boasts some unique plant species including prickly pear cactus and Canada yew (the only yew found in Manitoba). While paddling downstream, watch for river otters, muskrats, and turtles.

Archaeological surveys indicate that the area in which the park is located was home to Aboriginal populations several thousand years ago. Over the last century, the area has been frequented by trappers, loggers and miners. Paddlers can still observe remnants of those early resource harvesting activities. Since paddling the Manigotagan can take several days, backcountry campsites are located along the route.

While the Manigotagan River is road-accessible where it crosses Provincial Road 314 in Nopiming Provincial Park and PR 304 near the community of Manigotagan, the park itself is not road-accessible. Paddlers generally access the river from the PR 314 bridge, from Long Lake, or from Quesnel Lake — all of which are in Nopiming Provincial Park. Paddlers often exit the river at PR 304 or in the community of Manigotagan, just west of the park. ■

The park extends 45 kilometres along the river's length and reaches 750 metres from each riverbank, making it a long narrow park.

Manigotagan River

Manipogo

NAMED FOR THE SERPENT-LIKE LAKE MONSTER allegedly sighted several times throughout the twentieth century, Manipogo Provincial Park is a small, family-friendly, slightly off-the-beaten-path Lake Manitoba park. Do not let the park's namesake overshadow the natural beauty of this park. While the park's name may cause visitors to cast their eyes out over the water in hope, or dread, of a monster sighting, the most likely sights at Manipogo Provincial Park include families splashing about in the lake or gathering around campfires. Not to mention the sight of the aquamarine-coloured waters of Lake Manitoba itself.

Manipogo has a campground with almost 90 basic and electrical campsites, plus seasonal sites, a concession, and beach, all located on the sheltered waters of Toute Aides Bay near the north end of Lake Manitoba. The beach, although narrow, is long, providing lots of room for families to stake a spot on the shore. From the beach, follow a path to Conrad Point, which extends out into Lake Manitoba, to visit a popular bird-watching area. The park also has a boat launch on a channel in a marshy area that al-

Manipogo, the lake monster, has been described in local newspapers as an "enormous sheep-headed animal with a body 30 feet long and two feet thick, brownish in colour." Some reports noted one hump, other reports noted several. In the event monster-hunting is on your agenda, please take your camera. The existence of Manipogo has never been confirmed.

Manipogo Provincial Park is accessible via Provincial Road 276 about 60 kilometres north of Ste. Rose du Lac. It is one of five provincial parks on Lake Manitoba's shore — see also Lundar Beach, St. Ambroise Beach, Watchorn, and Margaret Bruce. ■

If monster hunting is on your agenda, please take your camera — the existence of Manipogo has never been confirmed.

lows boaters to launch in a sheltered spot before heading out onto the lake. Fishing from a dock by the boat launch also appears to be a favourite activity for many park visitors.

Officially established as a provincial park in 1961, Manipogo was first developed as a recreational area with a campground and other amenities in 1957, the same year that an expedition was launched to capture Manipogo.

Manipogo

Marchand

IF THE SIGN SAYS "Marchand Fire & Maintenance Base," then you have found the entrance to Marchand Provincial Park, located along Provincial Road 210 about nine kilometres east of the community of Marchand. The maintenance base is located behind the park. Like nearby Woodridge Provincial Park, Marchand became a park in 1974.

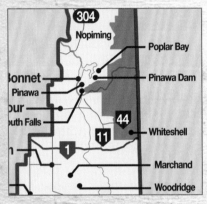

Marchand Provincial Park is located within the Sandilands Provincial Forest in southeast Manitoba. Descriptively named, the Sandilands area is part of a series of sand and gravel end moraine ridges deposited during the last period of glaciation. Jack pine forest dominates the area, but most of the original forest was destroyed by logging or forest fires by the early twentieth century. After the Sandilands became a federal forest reserve in the 1920s, re-seeding of Jack pine began. Thanks to several decades of seeding, much of the area today is once again covered with pine, along with blueberry and bearberry shrubs, mosses and lichens. Where soils are less sandy, the forest includes spruce, aspen and birch. Fire is still a danger, though, and a significant forest fire burned over 30 square kilometres of forest between Marchand and Woodridge in 2008.

At 0.02 square kilometres in size, Marchand Provincial Park is a day-use park with picnic tables and a picnic shelter. It serves as a staging area for hikers, cyclists, and cross-country skiers using trails of various lengths and difficulties in adjacent parts of the provincial forest. Cross-country ski trails are maintained by the Sandilands ski club.

Just south of Marchand Provincial Park, but still within the Sandilands Provincial Forest, is the Pocock Lake Ecological Reserve, a protected area that includes Pocock Lake and a beach ridge that is part of the Bedford Ridge. The reserve is named for Bill Pocock, a former Sandilands forest ranger. If the Sandilands Provincial Forest interests you, also visit the Sandilands Forest Discovery Centre located near Hadashville just south of the Trans-Canada Highway. ∎

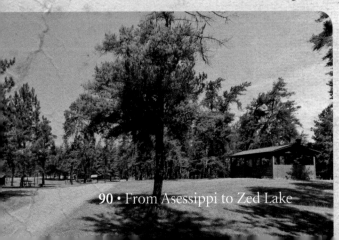

Margaret Bruce

MARGARET BRUCE PROVINCIAL PARK with its natural sandy beach is set against the aquamarine blue waters of Lake Manitoba. Margaret Bruce is one of only two provincial parks named after women (see also Patricia Beach on Lake Winnipeg).

Margaret (Maggie) Bruce was born Margaret Ann Anderson in Westbourne, Manitoba on May 10, 1881. On March 21, 1906, she married Samuel Bruce and the couple moved to Bluff Creek near Alonsa where they raised seven sons and one daughter. Their farm was adjacent to a natural beach along the west shore of Lake Manitoba. According to *Many Trails to Manitou-Wapah,* a local history of the area published in 1993, the beach "became a picnic and camping spot for the community. For years the only road to the lakeshore was through their property and the camping was on part of their land. Patiently, they endured gates being left open, allowing horses and cattle to escape."

Tragically, Margaret and two of her sons were killed in 1955 while enroute to her granddaughter's wedding in Portage la Prairie. After Margaret's death, the beach area was given to the local Legion and change rooms and bathrooms were built with the assistance of the province. The province acquired Margaret Bruce Park in 1958 and Margaret Bruce Provincial Park, 0.05 square kilometres in size, was designated in

1961. The park and campground are currently leased to a private operator.

Margaret Bruce Provincial Park is located at the end of a gravel road accessible just north of Silver Ridge on Provincial Road 278 not far from the community of Alonsa. On the way to or from the park, walk the three-kilometre Bluff Creek trail that follows the creek and loops around a marsh. The trailhead is on the north side of the gravel road. Margaret Bruce is one of five provincial parks on Lake Manitoba's shore — see also Manipogo, St. Ambroise Beach, Lundar Beach, and Watchorn. ∎

The natural sandy beach became a picnic and camping spot for the community.

Memorial Park

IN THE HEART OF WINNIPEG, AT THE HEART OF THE CONTINENT, lies a civic breathing space in the form of Memorial Park, a 0.02 square kilometre green space that honours the sacrifices of the Canadian military.

It is a park that almost never came to be, for in the late 1950s the City of Winnipeg was planning to build a new city hall at the intersection of Broadway and Memorial Boulevard opposite Manitoba's Legislative Building. The land had been owned by the provincial government, but it was promised to the city for the purposes of city hall construction. Along the east edge of the property, a

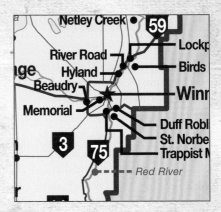

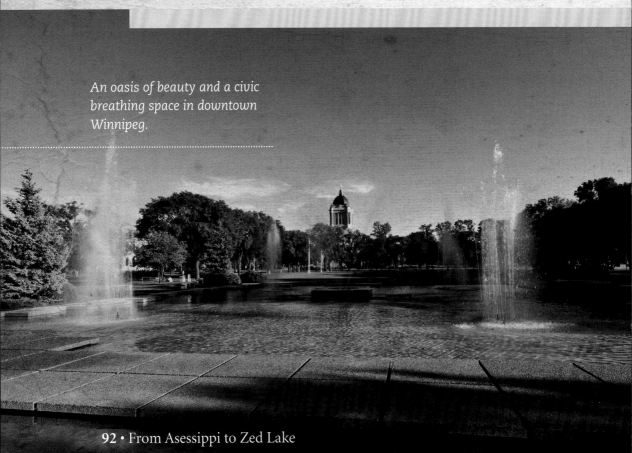

An oasis of beauty and a civic breathing space in downtown Winnipeg.

large cenotaph commemorating First World War casualties anchored Memorial Boulevard. Casualties of the Second World War, however, had not yet been commemorated in any way in Winnipeg — something Canadian Legion branches clamoured to rectify. The Legion petitioned Winnipeg's city council to create a memorial park rather than a city hall on the property in question. The Legion believed that a memorial park would enhance the dignity of the existing cenotaph.

Planning for a new city hall continued, while public support for a memorial park grew until Manitoba's premier, Duff Roblin, offered a substantial sum of money to the city to give up the Broadway site. After heated and sometimes acrimonious debate, the city agreed to accept the province's offer. It was to be a park, after all.

In 1961, the province announced that a decorative pool and fountain would centre the new memorial park. While some felt the price tag of the pool and fountain was steep, others felt that "long after the price tag has been forgotten, the fountain and pool will remain, an oasis of beauty in downtown Winnipeg."

Memorial Park became a provincial park in 1965. It features a manicured lawn, large shade trees, a pool and fountain, and numerous memorials. Within the park's boundaries are many monuments, including a statue of former Winnipegger Sir William Stephenson, "the man called Intrepid", spy and intelligence advisor to Sir Winston Churchill during the Second World War. A nearby statue commemorates women veterans of both world wars.

Memorial Park is located in downtown Winnipeg, bordered by Broadway, York, Osborne, and Memorial, with a small triangular piece of land where Memorial and Osborne converge. ■

Moose Lake

I T WAS ONCE OBSERVED THAT MOOSE LAKE appeared to be well-named as "magnificent specimens of moose flock to the lake shores in the early morning, and deer may be seen drinking the lake waters most any time of the day."

The railway reached Sprague in 1901 opening up the area to both farmers and the forest industry. By the early 1930s, settlers in the area began constructing a road to Moose Lake and fellow residents "donated food to feed the road builders, flour, hams, beans, bread, and the like." In 1932, the government surveyed the shores of Moose Lake for resort development. The area was described as "near perfection as anything on earth," where "even the trees seemed possessed of unusual vigour — birches of rare beauty, sturdy pines, tall-growing poplars." In 1954, a campground and picnic areas along Moose Lake were developed. A tourist camp followed in 1958. In 1961, Moose Lake became a provincial park. Today the park includes 90 cottages and its campground boasts 75 basic and electrical campsites.

Old beach remnants from glacial Lake Agassiz line the south and

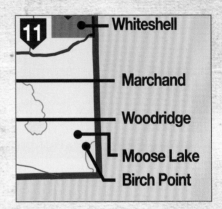

west shores of Moose Lake, marking the ancient lake's edge for a period of time. The area around Moose Lake also marks the western boundary of several eastern Canadian tree species including red and white pines, and white cedar. Look for signage along the east shore of the lake that marks a small two-hectare ecologically significant area with white and red pines, a remnant of a much larger pine forest that was decimated by the forest industry in the early twentieth century. Birch trees are noticeably present

Even the trees seem possessed of unusual vigour — birches of rare beauty, sturdy pines, tall-growing poplars.

throughout the park, and signage reminds visitors not to peel the birch bark.

Moose Lake is fairly shallow with a maximum depth of 5.5 metres and popular for both swimming and boating. A wheelchair-accessible fishing dock makes Moose Lake more accessible than many lakes.

For all the beauty of the Moose Lake area, for many, it has one striking advantage. Moose Lake is a short six-kilometre drive down a gravel road to Lake of the Woods. Birch Point, developed as a picnic site in 1960 and designated a provincial park in 1961, provides access to Buffalo Bay on Lake of the Woods. Anglers can

camp at Moose Lake or stay in a resort located within the park, and fish nearby on Lake of the Woods. Not surprisingly, due to its proximity to the United States border, Moose Lake and Birch Point are popular with both locals and Americans.

Moose Lake Provincial Park and its neighbour, Birch Point, are situated within the Northwest Angle Provincial Forest in the extreme southeast corner of the province. Access is either via a completely paved route that follows Highway 12 to Sprague, then Provincial Road 308 from Sprague to Moose Lake, or a partly gravel route that follows Highway 1 east, then PR 308 south to Moose Lake. ∎

Moose Lake

Neso Lake

VISITORS TO THE NORTHWEST PART of the province have no shortage of recreational options from which to choose. Many travellers on the highway between Cranberry Portage and Flin Flon may not even notice Neso Lake Provincial Park, not because Neso Lake has little to offer visitors, but because it is one of many picnic spots and boat launches along the route. The 50-kilometre stretch of Highway 10 between Cranberry Portage and Flin Flon provides access to Twin Lakes, Neso Lake, and Bakers Narrows provincial parks, as well as many other picnic areas.

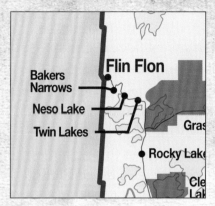

Neso, Cree for the number two, is the second in a series of numerically named lakes. Just south of Neso Lake is Payuk Lake, meaning "one". According to the Geographical Names Program, there are 14 numerically named lakes in the area.

For highway travellers, Neso Lake is a scenic rest stop and picnic area. For anglers, a boat launch provides access to the lake. For canoeists, Neso Lake is a starting point for the Mystik Creek canoe route. The route takes paddlers from Neso Lake past Nisto Lake and through a number of the small numerically-named lakes to Naosap Lake ("12" in Cree). From Naosap Lake, paddlers return through Alberts Lake into Lake Athapapuskow to Bakers Narrows.

Neso Lake is accessible via Provincial Road 621 from Highway 10, about 8 kilometres south of Bakers Narrows and about 17 kilometres north of Cranberry Portage. ∎

The recreational potential of this area was recognized by the late 1940s when, following the completion of Highway 10 in 1950, a recreational area approximately 29 kilometres by 48 kilometres between Cranberry Portage and Flin Flon was created and developed in the following decade. It quickly became a well-known fishing paradise with numerous lakes teeming with trout, walleye and northern pike. The area included 21 summer home subdivisions, many tourist camps, and several beaches. Neso Lake was included in this "scenic playground." A recreational area was established at Neso Lake in 1958, and a small area along the shore of Neso Lake became a provincial park in 1974.

Neso, Cree for the number two, is the second in a series of numerically named lakes.

Netley Creek

A 0.15 SQUARE KILOMETRE PARK is no match for Mother Nature when she is in spring flooding mode. If you drive north on Main Street in Winnipeg, and keep going, you will reach a small recreation park called Netley Creek Provincial Park. Main Street in Winnipeg becomes Highway 9 north of the Perimeter, and if you stay on Highway 9, it becomes Highway 9A also known as Main Street through Selkirk, then Provincial Road 320 north of Selkirk, also called Breezy Point Road. Just keep driving; no turns. Netley Creek Provincial Park is located at the end of the road, sometimes called the "End of Main," where Netley Creek flows into the Red River at the south end of the Netley-Libau Marsh. The park, however, is in transition. Park infrastructure including a much touted viewing tower and a privately operated campground is being removed, along with the entire Breezy Point cottage subdivision. A great marsh, but perhaps not so great a place for a park and cottages, due to repeated flooding and ice-jamming.

Park facilities or not, the Netley-Libau Marsh area remains popular for wildlife viewing, snowmobiling and angling.

Netley Creek became a provincial park in 1974, the same year that much of the southern province experienced widespread flooding. By mid-April in 1974, ice jamming on the Red River near Netley Creek had damaged 50 cabins at Breezy Point. A foreshadowing, perhaps, of many springs to come.

The Netley-Libau Marsh lands are made up of bays and channels including the Red River that flows through the marsh before emptying into Lake Winnipeg. In 1926, much of the area was reserved as public shooting grounds due to its abundance of waterfowl. Unlike Delta Marsh at the south end of Lake Manitoba that became well-known for its hunting lodges and celebrity hunters like Clark Gable, it was noted even in the 1920s that few duck hunters visited the Netley Marsh

area because of lack of accommodation. It was used mainly by resident hunters who "just wanted to have a good duck dinner at the start of the season." Park facilities or not, the Netley-Libau Marsh area remains popular for wildlife viewing, canoeing, and angling. The Red River between Selkirk and Netley Creek also remains a popular stretch of river for ice fishing in winter.

Netley Creek

Nopiming

WITHIN A STONE'S THROW OF WINNIPEG, or at least a relatively short car trip, is an ancient land carved and exposed by glaciers. A thin layer of soil supports the boreal forest, comprised of mosses, shrubs, a variety of conifers, and other plants. Despite the forest, the Precambrian Shield or Canadian Shield is largely a huge area of exposed rock. Nopiming, meaning entrance to or into the wilderness in Saulteaux, is part of this landscape. Located north of the Whiteshell and south of Atikaki, Nopiming's character also falls somewhere in the middle. It is less developed than the Whiteshell making it feel more remote, but more developed than Atikaki, which is a true wilderness park. Like Whiteshell and Atikaki, Nopiming is located along the Ontario border. Parts of Nopiming are included in the Manitoba-Ontario Interprovincial Wilderness Area (see Atikaki Provincial Park for more information on the wilderness area).

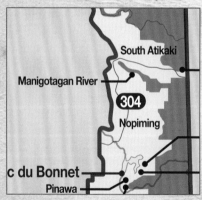

Nopiming became a provincial park in 1976 and is 1,429 square kilometres in size. If you arrive at Nopiming via Provincial Road 315, you reach a fork in the road just after entering the park. Continue on PR 315 to the right, and you will reach Bird Lake and Tulabi Falls. Take the left choice, which becomes PR 314, and you will travel up the length of the park to a number of lakes, campgrounds, and historic mining sites. One choice is not better than the other, just different. If you have time, try both.

The north part of Nopiming was part of the country that was home to Manitoba's first gold rush. By the early part of the twentieth century, prospectors were "turning the Precambrian Shield inside out in their random search for gold." Gold deposits at nearby Rice Lake where Bissett is located were first found by prospectors in 1911.

Several mines operated in north Nopiming in the 1920s and 1930s, including the Kitchener-Growler mine site along PR 304 near the north entrance of the park. Since gold in quartz veins was in low concentrations, the ore was processed at the mine sites rather than shipping it elsewhere. A cyanide process was used where a solution of sodium cyanide was added to crushed ore and lime, separating the gold from the ore. Tailings left over from the process formed "cyanide flats." At the Kitchener-Growler mine site, the ore also contained a small concentration of copper, and as a result, the flats have greenish-blue streaks, even today. The flats still remain relatively barren of vegetation. Interpretive signs along the highway also point to Wadhope, the townsite where many miners lived.

Cottage communities now occupy areas near former mine sites at Beresford and Long Lakes. Lots were also made available at Bird Lake in 1958, and a small provincial recreation park was established near Bird Lake in 1961. There are now almost 450 cottages in the park.

Nopiming is a paddler's paradise with a number of road-accessible designated canoe routes. Routes include Seagrim Lake, Rabbit River-Cole Lake, Bird River-Elbow Lake, and Beresford Lake-Garner or Long Lake. The Manigotagan River is also popular with canoeists and accessible via Caribou Landing in Nopiming (see Manigotagan Provincial Park for more information). Backcountry campsites are located along the canoe routes.

Nopiming

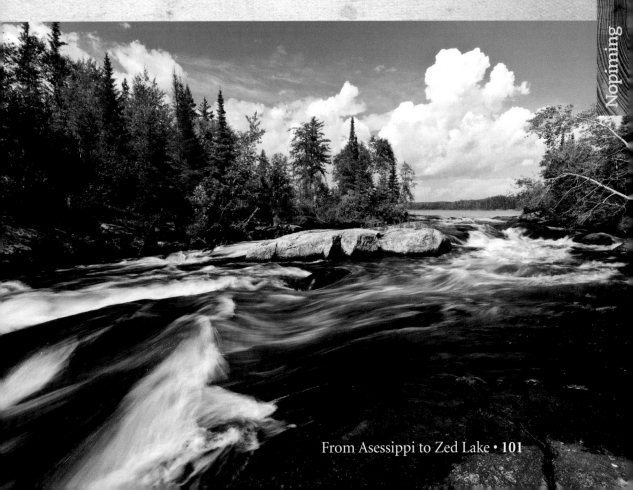

Nopiming

Nopiming is home to the southern-most herd of woodland caribou called the Owl Lake herd. To protect the caribou's calving area, access to an area around Flinstone Lake is limited during the summer. To view Flinstone Lake from afar, hike the 1.8-kilometre Walking on Ancient Mountains trail where you will get a glimpse of the lake from one of the trail's viewpoints. Walk to the farthest point on the trail for a view of Tooth Lake. For more information, a woodland caribou exhibit is located at Black Lake.

The 1.5-kilometre Fire of Eighty-Three trail, named for a forest fire that swept through the area in 1983, takes walkers through an area of re-growth. For a longer, more challenging hike, try the cairn-marked Black Lake trail leading from the Black Lake campground around the lake to the mouth of the Black River near PR 314. The trail is eight kilometres one-way if you leave a car at PR 314, or 16 kilometres return.

Campgrounds with over 130 campsites are located at Bird Lake, Tulabi Falls, Black Lake, Beresford Lake, and Caribou Landing. Just as all the roads in Nopiming are gravel, all campsites in Nopiming are basic non-electrical sites. The park is also home to a few private lodges. ∎

The north part of Nopiming was part of the country that was home to Manitoba's first gold rush.

Norris Lake

ONCE BILLED AS A PLACE where "the ducks quack and rise," Norris Lake in the south-central Interlake was known as a long narrow prairie lake filled with rice and prairie grasses on which ducks fed. In 1926, a writer in the *Free Press* noted that the country around Norris Lake was also well supplied with prairie chickens, just in the event any "palm-to-pine" hunters wanted to indulge in a couple of hours of shooting.

As a shallow lake, fish populations often experience winter kill due to oxygen depletion in water under the ice. After Norris Lake was first stocked with 2,700 rainbow trout in 1955, anglers were invited to catch their fill at the end of the season, since any trout remaining in the lake were not expected to survive the winter. Today, the lake is occasionally stocked with northern pike.

Norris Lake became a provincial park in 1974. Set among poplar and oak trees, a campground at Norris Lake has 15 basic campsites plus group use sites. The park's 0.09 square kilometre area also has picnic shelters, a boat launch, and a small beach.

Norris Lake Provincial Park is set in Manitoba's Interlake region about 20 kilometres northwest of the community of Teulon, and just east of the Shoal Lakes. While the southern Interlake is mostly agricultural, the remaining landscape is a mix of forest, meadows, wetlands, and shallow lakes. Once the floor of glacial Lake Agassiz, much of the area has a thin layer of soil underlain by limestone, which in places has

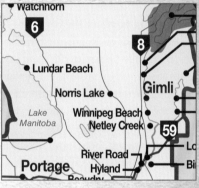

formed caves or sinkholes as a result of water percolating through the rock.

Visitors to Norris Lake may want to travel about 35 kilometres farther north to the Narcisse Wildlife Management Area to see more garter snakes than anywhere else in the world. In the spring the snakes emerge from limestone sinkholes and disperse to surrounding wetlands, returning to their dens in the fall. Walk a three-kilometre interpretive trail to learn more about the snakes.

To get to Norris Lake, travel north of Winnipeg on Highway 7 to Teulon, the follow Highway 17 west for 16 kilometres. ∎

North Steeprock

IF YOU MAKE IT TO BELL LAKE PROVINCIAL PARK, about 17 kilometres from Highway 10 on Provincial Road 365, you must travel another 17 kilometres up PR 365 to North Steeprock Lake Provincial Park. While the drive to North Steeprock Lake may not appear steep, your car engine will let you know that you are climbing. And while you may not notice the view on the way up, you will certainly see some fantastic vistas on your return trip back to Highway 10.

North Steeprock Lake is in the heart of the Porcupine Provincial Forest, one of the highest areas of the province just north of the community of Swan River. Road construction to the lake began in 1957, and a camping area adjacent to the lake was first developed in 1958. Designated a provincial park in 1997, the 0.13 square kilometre area is home to a picnic area, beach, boat launch, and a campground with 16 basic campsites, plus seasonal sites. Part of the campground is perched on a terrace above the lake. Archaeological excavations on the terrace area have uncovered artifacts from Aboriginal campsites several thousand years old. A cottage area is also adjacent to the park.

For anglers, the lake boasts northern pike, perch, walleye and whitefish. The campground at North Steeprock Lake can serve as a home base for anglers who might want to fish many of the other lakes in the area that contain a variety of native and stocked fish species.

And if you are wondering, there are virtually no similarities between

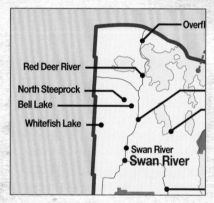

Steeprock, the recreational community on the east shore of Lake Manitoba, and North Steeprock Lake in the Porcupine Provincial Forest. One is a beach community somewhat Mediterranean in appearance, while the other is a deep clear lake in the forested uplands of the Porcupine Hills. Both however, are beautifully scenic.

North Steeprock Lake is one of three provincial parks in the Porcupine Provincial Forest — see also Bell Lake and Whitefish Lake. North Steeprock Lake is on Provincial Road 365 about 34 kilometres from Highway 10, just north of Birch River. ■

Part of North Steeprock's campground is perched on a scenic terrace above the lake.

North Steeprock

Nueltin Lake

PRENTICE G. DOWNES, A TEACHER FROM BOSTON, paddled up the Cochrane River to Nueltin Lake in 1939. Diaries of his journey with detailed entries, drawings, and the "remains of crushed mosquitoes" became the basis for *Sleeping Island: The Story of One Man's Travels in the Great Barren Lands of the Canadian North,* published in 1943. Describing Nueltin Lake's bewildering array of islands, he noted that in "every direction of the compass points, a vast maze as far as the eye could see. What was main shore, lakes, bays, islands, or points was all one endless confusion."

Steven Wintemute

Nueltin Lake, an island-filled lake that straddles Manitoba's northern border, takes its name from a Chipewyan word meaning "sleeping island". It is the largest lake in the area, with one third of its surface area in Manitoba, and the other two-thirds in Nunavut. The Thlewiaza River enters Nueltin Lake from the southwest and exits into Nunavut.

Eskers formed during the last period of glaciation when melt water channels or tunnels within glaciers became filled with sand and gravel. When the glacier melted, linear ridges of sand and gravel were deposited on the land. Many eskers wind across the northern Manitoba landscape, sometimes rising 50 metres above the surrounding area. The Robertson Esker, the longest continuous esker in Manitoba at about 190 kilometres in length, crosses the southeast part of the park.

The area is part of the winter territory for barren ground caribou that use the eskers as travel corridors. Grizzly bears, once indigenous to Manitoba but no longer found here, have been seen in the Nueltin Lake area. The area is also home to moose, black bears, lynx, other smaller mammals, and is part of the breeding habitat for many migrating birds. The area is also part of the winter habitat for rock ptarmigan.

Nueltin Lake Provincial Park takes its name from the lake. Designated a wilderness park in 2010, the park covers 4,472 square kilometres. The lake has, over the years, been popular for fly-in fishing, and many angling records have been established at Nueltin Lake. Canoeists who want to experience the true wilderness of the north also paddle the area's rivers. The area is part of the traditional territories of the Sayisi Dene and Northlands Denesuline First Nations who hunt, trap and fish in the area.

Nueltin Lake Provincial Park is not road-accessible. Access for fly-in fishing and canoeing can be arranged with lodges, outfitters, or air charter companies. ■

Nueltin Lake takes its name from a Chipewyan word meaning "sleeping island".

Numaykoos Lake

JUST EAST OF SAND LAKES PROVINCIAL PARK and southwest of Churchill lies Numaykoos Lake Provincial Park, designated as a provincial park in 1995. Not to be confused with Numakoos Lake, which lies west of South Indian Lake, Numaykoos Lake lies in the other direction. Both names mean "trout."

At 3,600 square kilometres in size, Numaykoos Lake is one of five large provincial wilderness parks set in northern Manitoba — see also Colvin Lake, Nueltin Lake, Caribou River, and Sand Lakes. The five cover over 25,000 square kilometres of northern Manitoba, contributing significantly to the total amount of protected areas in the province. All five parks are part of the winter range of barren ground caribou; animals that depend on undisturbed habitat to survive. Barren ground caribou migrate annually from northern tundra areas where they calve, to northern boreal forest areas where lichens allow the caribou to survive the harsh winters. Large, broad hooves allow the caribou to travel through snow or muskeg while allowing the animals to paw through the snow to find food.

Similar to other northern Manitoba parks, Numaykoos Lake lies in the transition area between boreal forest and tundra. The landscape, however, is relatively flat and covered by peat. Not unlike saturated soil that has dried and baked in the sun, the Numaykoos Lake landscape includes "frost polygons," multi-sided geometric shapes formed by repeated

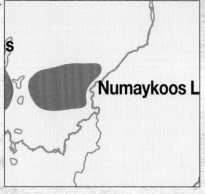

freezing and thawing of the surface that can take many decades to form. Sometimes called "tundra polygons," the natural shapes can be found in many parts of the arctic. The large polygonal shapes are often depressed in the middle and have uplifted edges. The shapes can be fairly large, and are most impressive when viewed from the air.

For paddlers, a small portion of the Little Beaver River passes through the southeastern corner of Numaykoos Lake Provincial Park before meeting the Churchill River on its way to Hudson Bay.

Numaykoos Lake Provincial Park is not road-accessible. Access can be arranged with lodges, outfitters, or air charter companies. ■

Oak Lake

LAKES IN SOUTHWESTERN MANITOBA are few and far between. When they do exist, they are much sought-after recreation destinations. Take Oak Lake, one of the bigger lakes in southwestern Manitoba, a remnant of a larger lake that formed as the last glacier retreated from the area about 12,000 years ago. The east side of the lake boasts a 0.11 square kilometre provincial park set in a much larger recreational community. The park itself has a beach, picnic areas, and a playground. It is adjacent to a large privately owned campground and surrounded by a community with more than 300 cottages, a marina, and other amenities.

Southwestern Manitoba, including the Oak Lake area, welcomed settlers in the late nineteenth century. Oak Lake was designated as a provincial park in 1961 and expanded in the late 1960s. In 1968, additional land for an access road, beach pavilion, and parking lot was acquired, and in 1969, some cottages were removed to expand the beach area.

According to the Manitoba Geographical Names Program, the lake was identified as "Oak Lake" on a mid-nineteenth century map, and named for the oak trees growing on its east shore. The recreational area is within the forested area, making it appear like a shady oasis on the prairie.

Historically, Oak Lake has been popular with anglers and was noted for its pike population. In dry years when water levels are low, fish populations are subject to winter kill. The lake is occasionally stocked with walleye.

Oak Lake, Plum Lakes, and surrounding marshes, form the Oak Lake-Plum Lakes marsh complex, a

popular bird watching area, especially during spring and fall migratory periods. A viewing area south of the provincial park at the south end of Oak Lake is a good place to see a variety of birds. The road and viewing area are on a beach ridge that separates Oak Lake from the Plum Lake marshes.

Oak Lake Provincial Park is situated southeast of Virden, about 12 kilometres south of the Trans-Canada Highway on Provincial Road 254. ∎

Overflowing River

PROBABLY THE LEAST WELL-KNOWN OF MANITOBA'S great lakes, Lake Winnipegosis is the province's second largest after Lake Winnipeg. It remains an important commercial fishing area. Interestingly, the northwest shore of Lake Winnipegosis has an abundance of salt springs and flats. Soil is saline, preventing much vegetation growth. You may see hues of red from iron oxides and even greens and oranges from micro-organisms. In the mid-1800s, the area was home to salt-making facilities, and salt was shipped via York boats down to Oak Point on Lake Manitoba, then by ox-carts to the Red River Settlement. Watch for the "salt flats" sign between Highway 10 and the lake.

The Overflowing River begins in the Pasquia Hills of Saskatchewan and flows into the northwestern tip of Lake Winnipegosis. By the time it reaches the lake, it has the appearance of a flat, full, peat-coloured river. With a name like Overflowing River, you cannot help but stand on the river's bank and wonder. And yes, records indicate that the name is descriptive as the river winds its way through low marshy ground and often overflows. To continue the theme, Overflowing River flows into Overflow Bay.

At 0.13 square kilometres in size, Overflowing River Provincial Park is a small park tucked into a large bend of the river near the river's mouth. First developed as a campground in 1957, it became a provincial park in 1961. The park itself is grassy with lots of shade trees and large spruce. Picnic tables and a small shelter provide visitors a lovely view of the river. The park and campground are currently leased to a pri-

vate operator. Access to the park is off Highway 10, between Swan River and The Pas — a stretch of highway that has few stopping points but some great views of Lake Winnipegosis.

For boaters, the park's boat launch near the mouth of the river provides access to Lake Winnipegosis, and it is the only provincial park with boat access to the lake. Just south of the park along Highway 10 is Red Deer River Provincial Park at the mouth of the Red Deer River, but while it has a picnic area, it does not have a boat launch. Birch Island Provincial Park, one of Manitoba's newest parks, is set in the middle of Lake Winnipegosis and is not road-accessible. ∎

Overflowing River

Paint Lake

DESCRIBED AS "A HUGE, BEAUTIFUL, island-studded lake," Paint Lake, the centrepiece of Paint Lake Provincial Park, is most definitely worth a visit, or better yet, several. Anyone travelling the length of the Grass River, or even part of it, would see the river twist and turn and generally wind its way in a north-east direction to eventually meet the Nelson River and Hudson Bay. About 45 kilometres upstream from Paint Lake, the Grass River tumbles over Pisew and Kwasitchewan Falls, after having slipped through Sasagiu Rapids. When the rough-and-tumble river reaches Paint Lake, it broadens and calms, providing a different kind of experience for visitors — one that is much more serene. Although a fairly large park at 227 square kilometres, most recreation development is confined to a small area on the lake's western shore.

Paint Lake Provincial Park is one of five provincial parks along the Grass River corridor — see also Grass River, Wekusko Falls, Sasagiu Rapids, and Pisew Falls. Of the five, Paint Lake is the farthest downstream. The

Grass River was part of the "upper track" fur trade route to Cumberland House in the late eighteenth century, just above the "middle track" Nelson River and the "lower track" Hayes River. In the 1790s the North West Company established McKay House on Paint Lake.

In 1961, access to Paint Lake was made possible for residents of Thompson by Inco (International Nickel Company of Canada) when the company created a trail to the lake. Although located on land leased to Inco by the province and not yet officially a provincial park, the area proved to be extremely popular with Thompson residents and the province responded by developing recreational facilities as early as 1962. The completion of Provincial Road 391 to Thompson in 1964 made the area accessible to all Manitobans. Paint Lake became a provincial park in 1971.

The Paint Lake campground, with over 70 basic and electrical campsites plus additional seasonal sites, is nestled among mature forest yet within close proximity to the lake. Regardless of your choice of campsite, the sound of loons may just lull you to sleep. Visit Dawn Beach in the morning or Twilight Bay in the evening for a swim in the refreshing waters of Paint Lake. Walk the scenic trail that stretches from the campground bays to the day use area for glimpses of the island-studded lake

at numerous points along the trail. Stop at Coffee Cove, but remember to bring your own coffee to sip while you enjoy the view.

For boating and angling enthusiasts, a marina is adjacent to a year-round resort. Paint Lake is also on the 725-kilometre Grass River Canoe Route. Due to the maze-like nature of the lake and its islands, boaters and canoeists should carry navigational aids.

More than 270 cottages are located in the park, and almost half of those are year-round residences. Due to the park's proximity to Thompson, many people choose to live along the beautiful shore of Paint Lake, and commute to Thompson for work and shopping.

About 32 kilometres from Thompson just off Highway 6 on Provincial Road 375, Paint Lake is popular in both summer and winter with campers, cottagers, cross-country skiers and snowmobilers. ■

Paint Lake

Patricia Beach

THE ATTRACTION OF PATRICIA BEACH PROVINCIAL PARK is simple — it is all about the beach. No fuss, no distractions, just a plain, natural white sand beach backed by small sand dunes. In contrast to Grand Beach, its much busier neighbour to the north, Patricia Beach offers peace and quiet, at least on most days. On sunny summer weekdays, visitors will feel like they have the beach almost to themselves. Even on weekends, it is still easy to claim a spot on the sand. Washrooms and a food concession are the only amenities in the park.

In the early part of the twentieth century, landowner George Allen built a cabin on his property near the lake that was used by family and as a hunting lodge. The land, however, was subject to periodic flooding when the lake was high, as it was in the mid-1950s. A 1958 report by the Lake Winnipeg and Lake Manitoba Flood Investigating Board recommended that the government purchase privately-owned lands affected by high stages of the lake. As a result, much of George Allen's property was acquired by the province in 1959. The purchase agreement between George and the province apparently stipulated that the new park would be named after George's only daughter, Patricia Joan Allen. In 1961, Patricia Beach Provincial Park was officially established, becoming one of only two provincial parks named after women (see also Margaret Bruce on Lake Manitoba).

Many think of Patricia Beach as the nudist, naturist, or clothing-optional beach, but if the thought of inadvertently walking into unclothed territory makes you avoid this beach, never fear. Nudists have their own piece of the beach at the far end of the peninsula, away from curious onlookers.

Located on the south-eastern edge of Lake Winnipeg along Balsam Bay about 70 kilometres from the capital city, Patricia Beach is easily accessible, even after a busy

Patricia Beach

The purchase agreement between George Allen and the province apparently stipulated that the new park would be named for George's only daughter, Patricia.

summer work day. Pack a snack and a towel, and plunk yourself down on the sand to watch a postcard-perfect sunset. Your blood pressure will thank you. To reach the beach, take Highway 59 north of Winnipeg to Provincial Road 319. ■

Pembina Valley

PEMBINA VALLEY PROVINCIAL PARK is full of oh-so-wonderful walking trails that will make your heart beat with exertion and your mind marvel at the beauty of the view. This small 1.8 square kilometre park is really all about walking, but pack a lunch as there are several picnic spots along the trail and a nice picnic area with a shelter near the parking lot. It is a day-use park only.

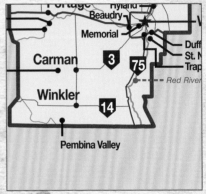

The park may be small in area, but it will feel a lot bigger once you hit the trail. Trails of various lengths and difficulties lead visitors up and down the valley walls through forests of oak and aspen. The longest trail, the 6.5-kilometre Pembina Rim trail, allows visitors to descend the valley wall, cross a creek in a couple of places, and reach the Pembina River at the trail's farthest point before crossing a deer meadow and looping back up to the parking lot. All trails lead to a scenic overlook or two that will give everyone a chance to take in the majestic view. As you walk the Pembina Valley, also keep your eyes on the sky. The valley is along a migratory route for red tailed hawks and other raptors that soar on thermal updrafts created when sun hits the valley's slopes.

The park may be small in area but it will feel a lot bigger once you hit the trail.

The Pembina River Valley is over two kilometres wide and about 100 metres deep. Only a few metres wide today, the river itself is a small trickle compared to what it would have been thousands of years ago when it filled the valley carrying huge volumes of glacial melt water. The river begins near the community of Killarney and flows in a southeast direction to meet the Red River near Pembina, North Dakota.

Prior to the park's designation in 2001, the land was privately owned by Henry and Elma Martens, who were interested in sharing the Pembina Valley with others. The family began clearing walking paths on their own initiative. The land was purchased by the province and the Nature Conservancy of Canada for the purposes of park creation.

Pembina Valley Provincial Park is south of Morden, about five kilometres east of Highway 31 on Provincial Road 201 near Windygates. ◼

Pembina Valley

Pinawa

DO NOT CONFUSE PINAWA PROVINCIAL PARK with Pinawa Dam Provincial Park. Just over ten kilometres apart, they are very different despite similarity in their names. The first is a practical rest stop and boat launch, while the other is a heritage park commemorating the province's first year-round hydroelectric generating station. Pinawa became a provincial park in 1974, followed by Pinawa Dam in 1985. Pinawa ranks as Manitoba's smallest provincial park at less than one hectare in size.

While Pinawa Provincial Park is functional rather than visually stunning like neighbouring parks Pinawa Dam and the Whiteshell, it is its placement on the landscape that is important, especially to boaters and anglers. Located adjacent to the Provincial Road 211 bridge just off Highway 11 about eight kilometres from the town of Pinawa, the park's boat launch provides access to the Winnipeg River downstream of the Seven Sisters Generating Station between Seven Sisters and Lac du Bonnet. From this point, boaters heading north can travel past Lac du Bonnet as far as McArthur Falls. Most of the land on this stretch of the river is privately owned. Boaters launching at the nearby town of Pinawa will be upstream of the Seven Sisters dam. The park also has picnic facilities with a view of the Seven Sisters dam in the distance.

PR 211, also called Pinawa Road, has been dubbed one of the best places in the province to observe Great Gray Owls. The expansion of neighbouring Whitemouth Falls Provincial Park to include land along PR 211 between Pinawa Provincial Park and the town of Pinawa protects an important staging and migration area for owls. Keep your eyes on the treetops for a glimpse of Manitoba's provincial bird, especially in winter, when the owls perch silently listening for prey. White-tailed deer are also plentiful in the area.

Pinawa is one of three provincial parks along the Winnipeg River — see also Whitemouth Falls and Whiteshell. ■

Pinawa

Pinawa Dam

PINAWA DAM HAS OFTEN BEEN COMPARED to Roman ruins. While this may seem an odd comparison for a site situated in the midst of eastern Manitoba's boreal forest, when you see the remains of this hydroelectric generating station, it is easy to see why the comparison is made. Although Pinawa Dam was constructed many years after the Roman empire, the imposing concrete and steel ruins topped with vertical concrete walls akin to columns has a kind of grandeur. The structure still spans the river's width, with water trickling through old chutes and crevices. Beautiful certainly, but also slightly forlorn.

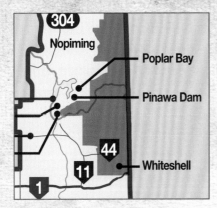

The Pinawa Dam opened in 1906 and transmitted power to Winnipeg and surrounding municipalities. To ensure enough water for year-round operation, the Pinawa channel was widened and dredged, and water was diverted from the Winnipeg River into the channel. The Winnipeg River, a favoured transportation route throughout the eighteenth and nineteenth centuries, became the favourite for electricity generation in the twentieth. Not long after the Pinawa Dam became operational, Pointe du Bois, Slave Falls, and Great Falls also boasted hydroelectric generating stations.

(left) The Pinawa Dam, first opened in 1906, was closed in 1951 so that the full flow of the river would reach Seven Sisters.

With the development of the "much greater and more important" Seven Sisters Generating Station near Pinawa on the main channel of the Winnipeg River, the Pinawa Dam was closed in 1951 so that the full flow of the river would reach Seven Sisters. In the late 1950s, militia engineers conducted demolition exercises with explosives at Pinawa Dam as the abandoned site provided "practice areas without equal in the province."

Fortunately, much of the dam's ruins still exist and provide a spectacular backdrop for a number of interpretive points of interest. Pinawa Dam became a provincial heritage park in 1985, commemorating Manitoba's first year-round hydroelectric generating station. Pack a picnic, and visit Pinawa Dam for an afternoon. The old townsite trail and the ruins trail give visitors a glimpse into the area's century-old history. Although swimming in the channel is not recommended, you will see many people playing in the rapids on a hot summer day. The Pinawa channel is also a favourite with canoeists.

Pinawa Heritage Park is along Provincial Road 520, which connects PR 211 (the highway to Pinawa) with PR 313 (the highway from Lac du Bonnet to Point du Bois). ∎

Pinawa Dam

Pisew Falls

STOP IN THE PARKING LOT AND PICNIC AREA of Pisew Falls Provincial Park and the thunderous sound of falling water immediately catches the ear, and the imagination. Perhaps you hear the hiss of a lynx? "Pisew" is the Cree word for lynx, and the falls have sometimes been called Lynx Falls. Follow the boardwalk down to the viewing platforms, and take in the sight of majestic Pisew Falls and the power and grace of tumbling water. Watch and listen as the Grass River tumbles 13 metres over rocks, then twists and whirls before making a sharp turn to head downstream. Spray from the falls contributes to lush greenery in the summer, and unique ice formations in the winter.

Although not recommended for safety reasons, for a heart-stopping close-up view of the falls, follow the beginning of the Kwasitchewan Falls trail over the suspension bridge and head up towards the top of Pisew Falls. Stand on the rocks immediately beside the deceptively smooth Grass River and watch it carelessly slip over the edge. An early 1960s guide to the Grass River canoe route cautioned paddlers that the falls are "neither seen nor heard until one is quite close to their brink." An amazing sight but parents watch your children.

Kwasitchewan Falls, the highest falls in Manitoba at 14.2 metres, can be reached via a 22-kilometre (return) backcountry hiking trail. While the trailhead is located in the Pisew Falls parking lot and picnic area, Kwasitchewan Falls themselves are not located in the provincial park. Pisew Falls, designated a provincial park in 1974, is fairly small at 0.93 square kilometres in size.

Pisew Falls Provincial Park is located along Highway 6 between Wabowden and Thompson. There are no campsites at Pisew Falls, but campsites are available in Paint Lake Provincial Park, about 50 kilometres away. Pisew Falls is one of five provincial parks along the Grass River — see also Grass River, Wekusko Falls, Sasagiu Rapids, and Paint Lake. ■

Poplar Bay

LIKE WEST HAWK LAKE AND LAKE ST. MARTIN, it is believed that Lac du Bonnet's Poplar Bay is a meteor crater lake. Although repeated glaciation over the millennia has altered the landscape and the level of the lake was raised by Manitoba Hydro in 1955 as a result of Winnipeg River hydroelectric development, in the 1970s a local graduate student in geology recognized the circular nature of the lake from a 1948 air photograph. Further study indicated that a meteorite about 160 feet in diameter likely hit the earth "sometime between 2.5 million and 2.5 billion years ago", creating a crater approximately 2,500 metres in diameter, about 750 metres deep, with an uplifted rim of about 100 metres in height. Depth contours in the bay are also circular in form, one of the features indicative of a meteorite impact.

Poplar Bay Provincial Park is midway between the town of Lac du Bonnet and Nopiming Provincial Park, on the eastern edge of Lac du Bonnet's Poplar Bay not far from where the Bird River enters the lake. A narrow inlet of Poplar Bay stretches toward Provincial Road 315, sometimes called Bird River Road, and the park is located on both sides of the inlet. Poplar Bay is a small 0.14 square kilometre park with over 30 cottages, a privately operated seasonal campground, store, boat launch, and beach. Named for poplar trees growing in the area, the "idyllic and peaceful" cottage community has been a popular tourist spot since the 1950s when Cornell Camp operated in the vicinity. It has the appearance of a mature and established cottage community where frenzied activity is non-existent during the long lazy days of summer. Poplar Bay became a provincial park in 1961.

To get to Poplar Bay, take PR 313 from the town of Lac du Bonnet (the highway to Pointe du Bois), to its intersection with PR 315. Follow PR 315 for about six kilometres. Poplar Bay is about 30 kilometres from Lac du Bonnet and 20 kilometres from Nopiming. ■

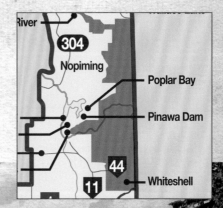

Portage Spillway

IN 1950, RED RIVER VALLEY COMMUNITIES, including the city of Winnipeg, were completely unprepared for a spring flood of massive proportions. It had been almost a century since the previous large flood occurred in 1861 and public awareness of such devastating events was low. The flood hit, and 100,000 Winnipeggers were forced from their homes. Following widespread damage, a federal-provincial royal commission made recommendations for flood protection schemes. The commission recommended construction of the Red River Floodway, the Assiniboine/Portage Diversion and the Shellmouth Reservoir.

(left) Not unlike a waterfall, the sound of the spillway draws attention as soon as you exit your car.

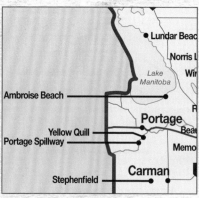

The Portage Diversion, sometimes called the Assiniboine River Floodway, is a 29 kilometre long excavated channel designed to divert water from the Assiniboine River north to Lake Manitoba. The diversion, completed in 1970, is part of the larger water management effort that begins with the Shellmouth Reservoir along the Assiniboine River in Asessippi Provincial Park.

The Shellmouth dam in Asessippi holds back water in the western part of the province, helping to control amounts that flow downstream into Brandon, Portage, and Winnipeg, and ultimately into the Red River. The Portage Diversion further helps to control amounts flowing into the Red River by diverting Assiniboine River flows into Lake Manitoba. The Portage Diversion includes a diversion dam in the Assiniboine River, a concrete spillway structure, and the channel itself.

Portage Spillway Provincial Park, located along the Assiniboine River just downstream of the diversion, was designated in 1997. Not unlike a waterfall, the sound of the spillway draws attention as soon as you exit your car. The 0.04 square kilometre park as the base of the spillway is a popular picnicking and day use area. Large river-bottom forest trees line the riverbank and provide shade for the picnic area. From the upper portion of the park, visitors can view the diversion dam. The park is also popular with anglers. Watch for pelicans, also fishing for their next meal near the spillway.

Portage Spillway is along the Yellowquill Trail, just south of the Trans-Canada Highway near Portage la Prairie. ■

Primrose

PRIMROSE PROVINCIAL PARK, at 0.06 square kilometres in size, is situated along the Birch River near the community of the same name. A wayside park for travellers well-stocked with picnic tables and shaded by tall deciduous trees, the park also has six basic campsites for overnight stays. Primrose became a provincial park in 1974.

A plaque on the north side of the park near the entrance, installed in 1995, commemorates Lake Agassiz. While the immediate connection to Birch River is not obvious, there is a link. Birch River is located immediately east of the Porcupine Hills, and the hills, part of the Manitoba Escarpment, would have formed the shoreline of glacial Lake Agassiz at one point in the distant past. As the lake receded, beach ridges formed when lake levels stabilized for a period of time. The plaque reminds us that not only did Lake Agassiz shape Manitoba's geography, it shaped our human history. Early aboriginal populations used Lake Agassiz beach ridges for "campsites, lookouts for sighting game, burial grounds, travel routes between seasonal camps, and sources of stone to fashion tools."

The first permanent settlers arrived in Birch River, described as a community "founded on a sand pile as a small lumbering centre," in 1910. Jack Hooke, an early Birch River teacher, described the area in those early days: "Not a road, not a bridge. All creeks and rivers running full tide all summer, and the land in between an unbroken series of undrained sloughs and swamps. The higher ground covered with poplar, spruce, and birch."

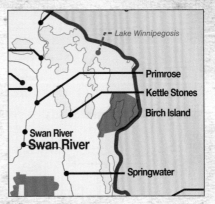

Enter the Primroses. Walter and Laura Primrose moved to Birch River from Ontario in 1911, homesteading on a quarter section that is now occupied by the community of Birch River. Walter worked for the T.A. Burrows Lumber Company which operated both north and south of the town, sold small parcels of land to other settlers, and trapped northwest of town. In 1944, the family moved to Fort William, Ontario. After Walter's death in 1947, Laura moved back to Birch River. Walter and Laura had 13 children. Some of their descendants still live in the Birch River area.

Primrose Provincial Park is along Highway 10 near the community of Birch River and just south of the intersection of Highway 10 with Provincial Road 365, the road to Bell Lake and North Steeprock Provincial Parks. ■

Primrose

Rainbow Beach

S ET IN A FLAT AGRICULTURAL PLAIN with Riding Mountain to the south and Duck Mountain to the northwest, Dauphin Lake is a shallow lake with a surface area of 500 square kilometres. It drains several rivers and creeks that originate in the Manitoba escarpment uplands. Settled in the late nineteenth century, the Dauphin Lake area was popular for both farming and commercial fishing. Communities in the area have long taken advantage of the abundant recreational opportunities like swimming, boating and fishing available at Dauphin Lake. There are several hundred cottages on the lake, most located near Dauphin Beach, Crescent Cove Beach and Ochre Beach.

In 1959, the diversion of Highway 5 near the communities of Dauphin and Ochre River and the purchase of land along the south shore of Dauphin Lake by the province allowed for a recreational development called Rainbow Beach. The name comes from Rainbow Creek, a small creek between Crooked Creek and Ochre Beach.

When the beach area was developed in 1960, a creek was

Rainbow Beach, 0.52 square kilometres in size, became a provincial park in 1961. Today, the park has a campground with over 70 basic and electrical campsites, seasonal campsites, group use camping areas, a concession, a playground, and baseball diamonds. A walking trail extends along the shore. The park's beach is long, and is one of many beaches along the shore of Dauphin Lake. A boat launch located along a creek in the park provides access to Dauphin Lake and is also popular with anglers fishing from a boardwalk across the creek. Dauphin Lake is stocked with walleye.

Rainbow Beach Provincial Park is located along Highway 20, about 18 kilometres east of Dauphin and just north of Ochre River. ■

dredged to make a boat channel and a long stretch of beach was cleared of rocks and boulders. The area was also lacking significant tree cover, so 2,000 trees were planted. By the time the beach was officially opened by Premier Duff Roblin in July 1960, it also included a 500-car parking lot, picnic shelters, a playground, and a small campground.

Rainbow Beach

Red Deer River

RED DEER RIVER FLOWS INTO AND OUT OF Red Deer Lake just north of the Porcupine Provincial Forest. After flowing out of Red Deer Lake, the river flows into Dawson Bay on Lake Winnipegosis. Along the east side of Highway 10 about 30 kilometres north of Mafeking near the river's mouth is Red Deer River Provincial Park, designated in 1974. And just north of Red Deer River Provincial Park along Highway 10 are the Lake Winnipegosis salt flats, a unique inland saline shore. Salt-making facilities that supplied salt to the Red River Settlement in the mid-1800s once operated in the vicinity.

In the early twentieth century, lumbering in the area provided the construction material necessary for the growth of settlements while also providing seasonal work for locals who were often engaged in summertime agricultural work. The south shore of Red Deer Lake was once home to the Union Lumber Company of Chicago. Between 1907 and 1926, it operated one of Manitoba's three largest lumber mills. The company employed 140 workers, processing about 20 million board feet of lumber annually.

Red Deer Lake and River are also an important part of the Lake Winnipegosis watershed, helping to maintain and influence water levels of the lake. From 1947 to 1964, Red Deer Lake was commercially fished. The Red Deer River, while not a significant walleye spawning river, is an important spawning channel for suckers from Lake Winnipegosis.

Highway 10 between Swan River and The Pas was completed in 1939. For drivers motoring to The Pas, crossing the bridge over the Red Deer River marked the end of continuous settlement, as the area to the north

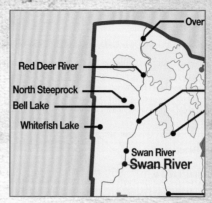

between the river and The Pas was only sparsely settled. It also marked the point along the route where, "for the first time, Lake Winnipegosis, with its magnificent expanse of water, may be glimpsed."

Red Deer River Provincial Park functions mostly as a highway rest stop and picnic area. Parks are used for many purposes, though. In 2010, Red Deer River served as a stopping point for First Nations individuals as they harvested sweet grass in the area. The grass was gathered, bundled, and braided; ready for ceremonial use at some later date. A picnic shelter and tables are located in the park's 0.01 square kilometre grassy area with views of the river. ■

River Road

THE FUR TRADE WAS WINDING DOWN and retired Hudson Bay Company men were granted lands along the Red, Assiniboine and Seine Rivers where they built homes and raised families.

River Road Provincial Park, designated in 1997, is a park in six pieces, consisting of small parcels of land connected by both the Red River and by Provincial Road 238, also known as River Road. Each parcel, like a piece of a jigsaw puzzle, reveals part of the Red River Settlement's story. The River Road Provincial Park sites are complemented by St. Andrew's Church (a provincial heritage site) and St. Andrew's Rectory (a national historic site) also located along River Road, and Lower Fort Garry (a national historic site), located just north of the park along Highway 9.

The entrance node at the south end of River Road high on a bank overlooking a sweeping curve of the river, along with the park's second site just farther north, introduce visitors to the river, its fish species, and the lifestyle of early settlers. The

Red River was designated a Canadian Heritage River in 2007.

The third, fourth and fifth sites mark stone houses built in the 1850s and '60s. Scott House, for example, gives visitors a glimpse into the limestone architecture of Red River. The house, only partially remaining, is evocative of old crumbling ruins in Europe, except on a much smaller scale.

A cairn and interpretive sign located on the east side of the road mark the fourth piece of the park. The cairn and sign refer to Twin Oaks, formerly Miss Davis' school for girls. Twin Oaks itself is privately owned and not part of the provincial park; only the roadside stop is part of the park. Up until the time Miss Matilda Davis taught school, Hudson Bay Company families sent their daughters to England for schooling. Miss Davis herself was a locally born daughter of a HBC officer who was educated in England before returning to teach in Red River. She taught French, music, drawing, dancing, needlework, and deportment — all skills required of English ladies in Red River.

Farther north, visit Captain Kennedy House — the fifth and most majestic piece of River Road Provincial Park — and former home of William and Eleanor Kennedy. William Kennedy led an eclectic life, spending time as an employee of the Hudson Bay Company, a missionary, and leader of an expedition to the Arctic in search of Sir John Franklin. Eleanor taught music at Miss Davis' school and made women's and children's clothing. The beautiful stone house contains a museum and tea room. A walk from the parking lot just south of the house takes visitors through formal gardens along the river.

The sixth and last stop marks the site where limestone was quarried to construct many of the stone buildings in the Red River Settlement, including St. Andrew's Church and Lower Fort Garry. An interpretive sign honours Duncan McRae, stonemason and master craftsman responsible for building many of the stone structures in Red River. The quarry is now a thriving marsh.

For non-history buffs, River Road offers angling opportunities, a tea room, strategically placed benches to contemplate the river and its surroundings, and a lovely drive past beautiful riverside homes. River Road Provincial Park is located on River Road, which intersects with Highway 9 about 10 kilometres north of Winnipeg. ∎

A heritage park in six pieces connected by both the Red River and by River Road, including the lynchpin of Captain Kennedy House

Rivers

THE RIVERS DAM, ABOUT 3 KILOMETRES east of the community of Rivers on the Little Saskatchewan River (formerly the Minnedosa River), was completed in 1960. The reservoir created by the dam is 610 metres wide at its widest point and 9.7 kilometres long. The reservoir is known as Lake Wahtopanah meaning "canoe people", and is sometimes called Rivers Lake. The impoundment was created as a water supply for Rivers and Brandon, for agricultural purposes, and for recreation.

Located about half an hour north of Brandon, Rivers Provincial Park, 0.86 square kilometres in size, was designated in 1961. Its campground has over 50 basic, electrical and full service campsites, as well as seasonal sites. The lower portion of the campground is adjacent to Lake Wahtopanah, while the remaining campsites are located farther up the reservoir's embankment. The park also has a large day use area with a beach, playground, picnic area and a concession. A boat launch provides access to the lake for angling.

For a glimpse of how the landscape appeared prior to settlement in the early 1900s, walk the Prairie Grass trail to check out the park's area of mixed grass prairie with big bluestem, harebells, gaillardia, and other prairie vegetation. The remnant prairie may have been slightly disturbed during the building of the dam, but it is nearly intact and it has never been ploughed. The Aspen trail will take walkers from the beach area to the community of Rivers.

Rivers Provincial Park is also a recommended place to begin a canoe trip down the Little Saskatchewan River to its confluence with the Assiniboine just west of Brandon. This 38-kilometre stretch of river drops 100 metres on its journey. Paddlers will experience some rapids and pass the site of Manitoba's first hydroelectric generating station that supplied electricity to Brandon for a couple of decades after its construction in 1900. The generating station operated for about eight months of each year.

To get to Rivers Provincial Park, take Provincial Road 664 for about three kilometres from the community of Rivers, or watch for signage along Highway 25 which connects Highway 10 north of Brandon to the community of Rivers. ∎

The reservoir is known as Lake Wahtopanah meaning "canoe people," and is sometimes called Rivers Lake.

Rivers

Rocky Lake

ROCKY LAKE, DESCRIPTIVELY NAMED to reflect the steep rock faces that line the lake's north shore, is centrally located between two well-known recreational areas, anchored by The Pas and Flin Flon at both ends and connected by Highway 10, once billed as the "high road to adventure."

North of Rocky Lake is the popular recreation area between Cranberry Portage and Flin Flon considered by many to be a scenic playground. The railway reached the mining community of Flin Flon in the late 1920s and miners and other travellers were the first to see the tourism potential of the surrounding areas. The community of Wanless near the shore of Rocky Lake was a railway point. Within a couple of decades, Highway 10 was constructed parallel to the railway in places, opening up the area to further development. South of Rocky Lake is Clearwater Lake Provincial Park, an area dubbed the new northern sports paradise when it was first developed for recreational purposes in the late 1940s and '50s.

Strategically located between the two larger areas, Rocky Lake, with a surface area of about 110 square kilometres and a maximum depth of almost 10 metres, is interesting in its own right. By the 1920s, the lake was commercially fished. It remains a popular angling spot for northern pike, walleye, smallmouth bass and whitefish. Recreational development at Rocky Lake, including a campground and boat launch, began in the mid-1950s. Rocky Lake Provincial Park at 0.24 square kilometres in size and located near the northeastern tip of the lake, was designated in 1961. Today, the park includes a public boat launch and a privately operated campground and resort. Many other cottages and year-round residences are located along the lake outside of the provincial park. Despite recreational development, the lake is quiet. Paddle a canoe to check out the lake's fascinating rocky shoreline, and you just may feel that you and the loons are the only creatures on the lake.

Rocky Lake is located about two kilometres west of the community of Wanless along Provincial Road 629. Wanless is located along Highway 10 about 45 kilometres north of The Pas. ■

Strategically located between Flin Flon and The Pas, Rocky Lake is interesting in its own right.

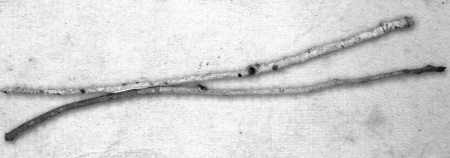

St. Ambroise Beach

St. Ambroise Beach allows visitors to appreciate both sides of the sand barrier ridge - the beach and the marsh.

ST. AMBROISE BEACH IS ONE OF SEVERAL Lake
Manitoba provincial parks within easy driving distance
of Winnipeg, and within even closer proximity to Portage la
Prairie. Compared to the popularity of Lake Winnipeg beaches,
Lake Manitoba beaches tend to fly under the radar of most
beach-goers, resulting in fewer crowds, and more of a getting-
away-from-it-all feeling.

Officially designated as a provincial park in 1961, St. Ambroise Beach was first developed as a recreation area with a campground and other amenities in 1957. Situated on a sand barrier separating Lake Manitoba from Sioux Pass Marsh, St. Ambroise Beach allows visitors to appreciate both sides of the ridge — the marsh and the beach. The sand ridge is stabilized by a variety of trees including willows, Manitoba maples, green ash and cottonwoods. Picnic areas, a playground, and a boat launch line the long narrow stretch of beach. Many sand "islets" lay just off shore.

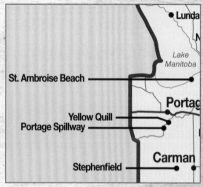

On the Sioux Pass Marsh side of the park, a short self-guiding trail in the marsh leads to a look-out tower. Several interpretive points along the boardwalk trail reveal information about the marsh and its inhabitants. The marsh is part of the larger Delta Marsh complex that stretches along the southern edge of Lake Manitoba. The beach along Clandeboye Bay just south of St. Ambroise Beach has been designated a "Special Conserva-tion Area" to protect piping plover habitat, and is closed to the public between April and August. The Clandeboye Bay Special Conser-

vation Area, one of three special conservation areas in the province, was first set aside for breeding piping plovers in 1983.

St. Ambroise Beach provides a unique camping experience for campers who enjoy being close to water, with the lake literally steps away from most of its 120 basic and electrical campsites. Unlike most other provincial park campgrounds where campsites are grouped togeth-er in clusters, St. Ambroise campsites are arranged in a long linear fashion along the shore.

To get to St. Ambroise Beach, take Highway 1 west of Winnipeg to Provincial Road 430 near Oakville. Travel north on PR 430 past the town of St. Ambroise, to St. Ambroise Beach. Alternatively, take PR 411 from Woodlands along Highway 6. ■

St. Malo

THE RAT RIVER BEGINS IN THE Sandilands Provincial Forest in southeast Manitoba and winds in a north-westerly direction to flow into the Red. In 1959, a dam was constructed on the Rat River near the community of St. Malo, primarily for water conservation purposes. A reservoir of water would help to provide a more reliable flow downstream and it could be used for agricultural purposes as well as future municipal water for the communities of St. Malo, St. Pierre, and Otterburne. As with other water impoundments in southern Manitoba, the St. Malo reservoir also opened the door to recreational development.

St. Malo is nicely designed to accommodate the variety of recreational opportunities it offers while retaining a natural atmosphere.

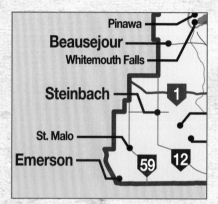

St. Malo Provincial Park was designated in 1961. At 1.5 square kilometres in size, St. Malo is nicely designed to accommodate the variety of recreational opportunities it offers while retaining a natural atmosphere. Set in the eastern Red River Valley, the area's mix of aspen/oak forest and prairie are reflected throughout the park. Located about 50 kilometres south of Winnipeg, family-friendly St. Malo is a hive of activity during the summer due to its proximity to the city and many other communities in southeast Manitoba.

Over 400 basic and electrical campsites are available for campers. Part of the campground is set in the park's forested area providing campsites with more privacy, and part of the campground is set along the east shore of the reservoir in a more open setting. A concession is also located within the park near the beach.

Walk the Tallgrass Parkland trail, a grassy trail through the park's aspen and oak forest that takes visitors to a couple of small tall grass prairie remnants along the park's northern boundary. The Trans Canada Trail also enters the park on its east boundary, and exits on its west. In winter, try the park's cross-country ski trails.

The park's central feature is St. Malo Lake with its two good-sized sandy beaches. Rent a paddle boat or toss in a canoe or kayak for a leisurely exploration of the reservoir. Powerboats are not allowed. Walk along a path from the parking lot near the park's entrance to the dam, and watch the Rat River slide over the dam to continue its journey toward the Red River. Interpretive signage near the dam explains the dam's history. The river downstream of the dam is a popular spot for angling.

St. Malo Provincial Park can be reached via Highway 59 south of Winnipeg to the community of St. Malo. The park entrance is just east of the highway. ◼

St. Malo

St. Norbert

PICNIC IN SOUTH WINNIPEG WHERE THE eastward flowing La Salle River meets the Red and explore the Aboriginal, Metis and French Canadian heritage of St. Norbert.

Aboriginal, Metis and French heritage mingle in St. Norbert.

A spearhead found near the La Salle River dates Aboriginal use of the area to several thousand years ago. At another site along the Red River not far from the La Salle, pottery over 1,200 years old was found. It is believed that these early peoples frequented the area on a temporary and seasonal basis (see Lockport Provincial Park for more detail on early Aboriginal populations).

By 1825, the Red River Settlement reached as far south as the La Salle, and this part of the settlement was occupied by mostly French-speaking Metis. For many years, the area was a rallying point for spring and fall buffalo hunters before they headed out onto the prairie. In the late 1850s, the parish of St. Norbert was created, named after the first bishop of St. Boniface, Joseph Norbert Provencher. Also by this time, Red River carts were plying the Pembina Trail between the Red River Settlement and the south. By the 1860s, many residents of the area were caught up in the challenging political times surrounding the Riel Resistance and the emergence of Manitoba as the first western Canadian province in 1870.

After 1870, immigrants began arriving in the area, including French Canadians Joseph Turenne, who built a two storey log home in 1871,

and Benjamin Bohemier, who built a barn-shaped "gambrel-roofed" home in 1889. By the turn of the century, St. Norbert had transitioned from a predominantly Metis community to a French-speaking agricultural community.

Plans for a heritage park began when the Turenne and Bohemier houses were saved from demolition and donated to the province. St. Norbert Provincial Park, a heritage park designated in 1976, includes the restored Turenne and Bohemier houses. The park also includes the un-restored Metis "Red River frame" Delorme house, and Henderson House, an early building from the Red River Settlement. Interpretive tours are available in the summer. Also within the park's boundaries are a picnic site and a one-kilometre walking trail that takes visitors along the La Salle River to its confluence with the Red.

St. Norbert Provincial Park is located along Turnbull Drive, just east of Highway 75 in the St. Norbert area of Winnipeg. ■

St. Norbert

Sand Lakes

MANITOBA'S LARGEST PROVINCIAL PARK at 8,310 square kilometres, Sand Lakes Provincial Park, designated in 1995, is part of the gently undulating northern Manitoba landscape with glacial landforms, exposed bedrock outcrops and many small lakes. Similar to the other northern parks such as Numaykoos Lake, Caribou River, Nueltin Lake, and Colvin Lake, Sand Lakes is located in the transition area between boreal forest and tundra. And like the other northern parks, Sand Lakes is part of the esker landscape. As the last glacier melted, sand and gravel carried in its drainage channels were deposited on the surface of the ground, sometimes rising up to 50 metres above surrounding areas.

Taking its cue from the esker landscape, the largest lake in the park is descriptively-named Big Sand Lake at about 113 kilometres in length. Much of the lake's shoreline is indeed sandy. Popular with fly-in anglers and home to a privately owned lodge, the lake is known for northern pike, lake trout, walleye, and arctic grayling.

Big Sand Lake is part of the South Seal River canoe route. The canoe route begins near the southwest tip of the park then continues through Big Sand Lake, Loon Lake, and Chipewyan Lake, all within the provincial park. The canoe route then continues down the South Seal River to where it meets the north branch of the Seal River at Shethanei Lake, just northeast of Tadoule Lake. From Shethanei Lake to Hudson Bay, the Seal River is a Canadian Heritage

Manitoba Conservation, Parks and Natural Areas Branch

Taking its cue from the esker landscape, the largest lake in the park is descriptively-named Big Sand Lake.

River, designated in 1992.

While the Seal River was never a main route during the fur trade era, it was used by Aboriginal populations for hunting, fishing and travel. Peter Fidler, Hudson Bay Company trader, explored the Seal River from Fort Churchill upstream, discovering that it began near Southern Indian Lake, part of the Churchill River system.

The park is home to moose, bear, wolves and many other mammals. Similar to the other northern parks, Sand Lakes is also part of the winter range for barren ground caribou. The park is also home to many kinds of waterfowl and shorebirds, containing a significant Caspian tern breeding area.

Located north of Thompson and northeast of Lynn Lake, Sand Lakes Provincial Park is not road accessible. To fly into Sand Lakes, arrangements can be made with lodges, outfitters, or air charter companies. ■

Sasagiu Rapids

FOR TRAVELLERS ON HIGHWAY 6 NORTH TO Thompson, Sasagiu Rapids is mostly a highway rest stop. But what a rest stop. After travelling through many kilometres of dense boreal forest, drivers motoring by on the highway might be tempted to step on the brakes at the sight of the wide swath of rapids, and rightly so. The Grass River, passing through Setting Lake, slips through Sasagiu Rapids before heading northwest to tumble over Pisew Falls and Kwasitchewan Falls a few kilometres downstream. The highway bridge crosses right over the rapids, making for scenic views on both sides of the highway.

Visitors who stop to take a closer look are greeted by the sound of rushing water as soon as the car doors are opened. Follow the sound created as the river drops almost four metres. Paths on either side of the highway lead down to water level where large glacier-scoured, multi-coloured rocks frame the rapids. With a little bit of rock-hopping, the rapids are close enough to touch. The river narrows as it roars under the highway bridge, but widens on the opposite side once again. Although not recommended for safety reasons, it is also possible to walk under the bridge, rather than climbing up the highway embankment to get to the other side. Fur traders travelling the Grass River "upper track" trade route to Cumberland House portaged these rapids, walking the same rocks as visitors scramble over today. If checking out the rapids on foot, be careful. In the Cree language, the name Sasagiu means "where fast flowing water runs through slippery rocks."

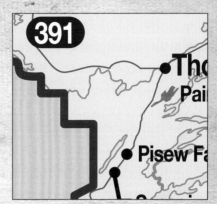

At about one square kilometre in size, Sasagiu Rapids Provincial Park includes both land and water. A boat launch provides access to Setting Lake. Anglers also dot the shore, hoping to catch walleye and northern pike. The park and campground are leased to a private operator.

Sasagiu Rapids, designated as a provincial park in 1974, is one of five provincial parks along the Grass River corridor — see also Grass River, Wekusko Falls, Pisew Falls, and Paint Lake. ■

Seton

DESPITE ITS LOCATION RIGHT ALONG the Trans-Canada Highway just east of Carberry, most travellers would not recognize this small 0.02 square kilometre wayside park for what it really is – Seton Provincial Park. Situated where the highway crosses Pine Creek, the park has also been known as Pine Creek Park. Established in 1958 as a wayside park, it was named for Ernest Thompson Seton in 1960 to commemorate the 100th anniversary of his birth. The park was then designated a provincial park in 1974.

Born in England, and raised and educated in Ontario, Seton arrived in Manitoba in 1881 at the age of 21, joining his brothers on their homestead near Carberry. He roamed the wilderness, studying birds and animals in their natural habitats. His talents as both an artist and writer resulted in the publication of *Mammals of Manitoba* in 1886 and *Birds of Manitoba* in 1891. In recognition of his knowledge and appreciation of nature, he was appointed Manitoba's naturalist in 1892, a position that was largely honorary. Seton travelled extensively in both Europe and the United States, spending the latter part of his life in New Mexico. In conjunction with Lord Baden-Powell and Daniel Beard, he is credited with establishing the Boy Scouts of America in the early twentieth century.

A prolific writer, Seton published many books and thousands of articles. His 1898 publication *Wild Animals I Have Known* brought Seton international fame. One of his stories that publicized the Carberry sand hills area to the world, *Trail of the Sandhill Stag* (1899), was first published in 1886 as a *Forest and Stream* magazine article called "The Carberry Deer Hunt." The story exemplified Seton's expertise at the "realistic animal story" literary genre, a genre also occupied by Seton's contemporary, *Jungle Book* author Rudyard Kipling.

Seton Provincial Park occupies a tiny part of the Assiniboine River Delta, an area that was formed where the Assiniboine River emptied into glacial Lake Agassiz (see also Spruce Woods Provincial Park). The park functions as a highway rest stop and picnic area between Sidney and Carberry. It is accessible from the westbound lanes of the Trans-Canada Highway. A plaque near the entrance honours the park's namesake. ■

South Atikaki

TUCKED BETWEEN ATIKAKI (pronounced a-tick-a-tkee) and Wallace Lake along the Ontario border is South Atikaki Provincial Park. Part of the beautiful and ancient Precambrian Shield, South Atikaki's landscape is home to glacier-scoured exposed rock, numerous lakes and wetlands, and boreal forest. "Atikaki" means country of the caribou, and small numbers of woodland caribou, a threatened species in Manitoba, live in the region.

Historically, the Wallace Lake area was part of Manitoba's early twentieth century mining boom when gold and other minerals were discovered in the Wanipigow River watershed and in other nearby areas. By the mid-1920s, over 80 mineral claims had been staked in the Wallace Lake area. The area is still a centre of mining activity today. It is this activity that precipitated some park boundary shifting in the mid-1990s.

The 140 square kilometre area now encompassed by South Atikaki was once part of Atikaki Provincial Park, designated as Manitoba's first wilderness park in 1985. The wilderness park classification, however, is for purposes of conservation and does not allow for mining, petroleum, or hydroelectric developments. As noted, the southern portion of Atikaki contained several mineral claims, an inconsistency with the park's wilderness classification. Rather than changing the classification of Atikaki, the park's boundary was adjusted by removing the south area from Atikaki and designating it as South Atikaki, first as a park reserve, then as an independent provin-

cial park in 1997. South Atikaki was given a natural park classification; a classification that allows resource development.

While there are no roads into South Atikaki, the park includes Wallace Lake itself, making it accessible by water from Wallace Lake Provincial Park on the lake's south shore. Wallace Lake Provincial Park can be reached via Provincial Road 304. If paddling through South Atikaki into Atikaki, the recommended route begins at Wallace Lake then heads east to Siderock Lake before following the "infamous" very difficult 5-kilometre long portage through South Atikaki that crosses a creek and two small lakes, before reaching Obukowin Lake in Atikaki. ■

Springwater

SPRINGWATER PROVINCIAL PARK along Highway 10 just north of Ethelbert between Pine River and Sclater is the only provincial park descriptively named for a local source of spring water. A spring located in a ravine along Highway 10 had been a public source of water for many years, since some groundwater in the district was of poor quality. A wayside park developed in the vicinity of the spring, and in 1964, Springwater became a provincial park. In 1987, the government installed a pump to bring the water closer to the highway where locals and tourists could access the water more easily.

When the community discovered that their spring water was to be privatized, hundreds signed petitions. In 1998, a colourful debate in the Legislature regarding proposed privatization of the water source for bottling purposes occurred. The Member of the Legislative Assembly for the area, while defending the right of community residents to access this source of drinking water, declared that people came from afar for the water "because they say that this is the best water for making dill pickles." A portion of the park was leased to a bottling facility that operated from 2000 to 2006. The facility no longer operates in the area.

Springwater Provincial Park is 0.18 square kilometres in size, and located on both sides of Highway 10 about nine kilometres north of Pine River. On the east side of the highway is the former wayside park. Park facilities no longer exist, and the park is in the process of re-vegetating. Immediately north of the former picnic area is a small parking area on

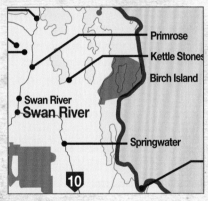

the side of the highway. A concrete staircase from the parking area leads down to a spring that flows out of the side of the ravine. Water continually flows, trickling further down the ravine to join a stream. There are no signs pointing to Springwater Provincial Park, but if you reduce your speed and keep an eye on the side the highway, you will see evidence of where the park is still located. ■

"They say that this is the best water for making dill pickles."

Springwater

Spruce Woods

DRIVING ALONG THE TRANS-CANADA HIGHWAY between Portage la Prairie and Brandon, the landscape changes dramatically. Grassy hills and scattered spruce appear suddenly as the flat prairie is temporarily left behind. It is a welcome change in scenery for anyone passing by. For those who choose to stop and take a closer look, it is an area where sand dunes and cacti are juxtaposed with meandering creeks and towering white spruce.

For all its marvellous vegetation and unusual sandy landscapes, Spruce Woods is a place of water, or at least a place created by water. Twelve thousand years ago the Assiniboine River, much larger than it is today due to melt water from glaciers, emptied into Lake Agassiz. Sand and gravel carried by the flowing waters were deposited where the river entered the lake, forming the landscape still known today as the Assiniboine River delta. Since that time, the river has continued to carve and twist its way through the land, creating spectacular sandy cliffs and vistas for those individuals lucky enough to be paddling gently downstream. Today of course the Assiniboine River is much smaller and more serene.

Spruce Woods Provincial Park, located just south of the Trans-Canada Highway near Carberry, covers a small area of the Assiniboine River delta. The park was established in 1964 and expanded in 1975 to include the Bald Head Hills, now also known as the Spirit Sands. Prior to its designation as a provincial park, Spruce Woods was a forest reserve established by the federal government in 1895.

In 1806, fur trader Alexander Henry called the sandhills "Devil's Mountain" in reference to strange noises and unusual apparitions. Early settlers avoided the unusual terrain. For Aboriginal people, the hills allowed them to be close to the Great Spirit, "Kiche Manitou", rather than being an area to fear. If names help to create a sense of place, then names like Spirit Sands, Devils Punch Bowl, Hogsback, and Kiche Manitou must make many wonder at the mysterious nature of Spruce Woods Provincial Park.

One could be forgiven for thinking that they were at Grand Beach while walking the dunes of the Spirit Sands. After glacial waters receded thousands of years ago, winds shaped the delta sand into spectacular sand dunes. Today, sand covers an area within the park only four kilometres square, much smaller than the 6,500 square kilometres of open sand that existed 8,000 years ago after Lake Agassiz receded. But even with encroaching vegetation, the dunes are still impressive. Canada Post commemorated the sand dunes in a series of provincial and territorial park stamps, issued to celebrate Canada Day in 1993. Although not a true desert as the area receives too much precipitation every year, the dunes can feel like a desert on a hot prairie summer day. An interpretive centre and walking trails through the Spirit Sands help visitors to understand the evolution of the dunes and their significance to aboriginal people. If walking the dunes, remember to carry drinking water.

Adjacent to the Spirit Sands, a trail leads to the Devils Punch Bowl

After glacial waters receded thousands of years ago, winds shaped the delta sand into spectacular sand dunes.

Spruce Woods

— a bowl-shaped depression with a small blue-green pond at its base. Underground streams in the area have caused collapse of the sandhills, creating this unusual feature. Catch a glimpse of the amazing countryside from a scenic lookout above the punch bowl. Further east along the river, the Hogsback is also an area affected by underground streams.

East of the Spirit Sands, visitors can appreciate a vastly different landscape. Epinette Creek, spring-fed and flowing all year, has a certain charm as it meanders its way to eventually meet up with the Assiniboine. Simple wooden bridges span the creek in several locations, helping to bring the creek up close and personal to those on the Epinette Creek trail. In summer, walkers and cyclists use the trail, while in the winter, it is an excellent cross-country ski trail. During the fur trade, Pine Fort (Fort Epinettes) was once located near the junction of Epinette Creek with the Assiniboine, and then re-located nearby in a later period of its history.

The Isputinaw trail takes visitors from the campground through a riparian floodplain area, while the Marshs Lake trail introduces visitors to an oxbow lake. The Trans Canada Trail also traverses the park, beginning in the southeast corner and crossing the park diagonally.

Spruce Woods is home to northern prairie skinks, Manitoba's only lizard. A typical skink measures no more than 20 centimetres from head to tail. When threatened, the skink will lose its tail, which keeps

Spruce Woods is a place of water, or at least a place created by water.

wriggling for several minutes after the skink has escaped. The skink will soon grow a new tail. They make their home in mixed-grass prairie areas with clumps of junipers, burrowing into the sandy soil below the frost line in winter. With forest species like aspen moving into the grasslands, the skink's preferred prairie habitat is shrinking, making it an endangered species.

The Assiniboine Delta area was also home to Ernest Thompson Seton for a period of time. As a young man living near Carberry, Seton explored the Spruce Woods area on foot, recording his observations of the natural world in articles and books read by people all over the globe. In 1940, many in the delta area wanted to change the name of the forest reserve to commemorate Seton, while others wanted to commemorate another famous naturalist from the area — Norman Criddle. While the "Spruce Woods" name was maintained when the forest reserve finally became a provincial park, both Seton and the Criddle family were commemorated in other ways (see Criddle/Vane Homestead Provincial Park and Seton Provincial Park).

In close proximity to Brandon, visitors can easily enjoy spending a day exploring the park. For those who would like to spend more time, Kiche Manitou campground offers over 160 basic and electrical campsites, as well as furnished yurts.

Spruce Woods is located on both sides of Highway 5 between Carberry and Glenboro. ■

Spruce Woods

Stephenfield

THE CREATION OF RESERVOIR LAKES IN THE MIDST of the prairies seems to go hand-in-hand with park development. Reservoir parks are not uncommon in southern Manitoba — Asessippi, Rivers, St. Malo, and Stephenfield are all provincial parks located on reservoirs. Reservoirs or im-poundments created by the damming of rivers often provide enhanced boating, angling and swimming opportunities in ways that regular riverbank parks do not.

Stephenfield Provincial Park, designated in 1971, is on the south shore of the five-kilometre long res-ervoir created by the damming of the Boyne River just west of Carman in the late 1960s for water conservation purposes. Set in a mostly agricultural area, this attractive park is pleasantly treed with aspen and oak. Watch for deer browsing among the vegetation.

The park is set within the larger Ste-phenfield Game Bird Refuge, a desig-nation that disallows anyone to hunt, take, kill, capture, retrieve or possess a game bird within its boundaries.

This family-friendly park's 0.94 square-kilometre area is packed with things to do, but because the park stretches along the reservoir's shore, it has a feeling of spaciousness. The

park has a beach and playground, picnic areas, boat launches, and other areas for various sports and games. Its campground has over 140 basic, electrical and electrical/water campsites, plus yurts located right along the reservoir's shoreline very near the beach. The park also has seasonal and group use campsites.

More than ten kilometres of walking trails cross the park and many trail segments parallel the reservoir's undulating shore. Most trail segments are named after birds — bluebird, tanager, goldfinch, and bobolink. The Bobolink trail leads to the Stephenfield Dam and Spillway just beyond the east end of the park, a favourite point of interest with many visitors and anglers. Watch the Boyne River slide down the spillway before continuing on its eastward journey. On the opposite side at the west end of the park, walk the 2.5 kilometre, descriptively-named "Surviving This Harsh Climate Self-guiding Trail."

Stephenfield is located about an hour's drive southwest of Winnipeg. To get to Stephenfield, take Highway 3 to Carman, then Provincial Road 245 for about 23 kilometres west of Carman. Turn north at the park signs. ■

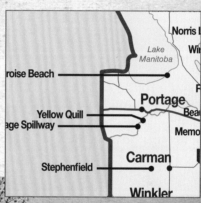

Swan River

THE SCENIC SWAN RIVER VALLEY stretches about 40 to 50 kilometres across, slicing neatly through the Manitoba Escarpment with the Porcupine Hills to the north and the Duck Mountains to the south. Most of the valley lies within Manitoba, although part extends into Saskatchewan. From the late eighteenth century to the early nineteenth, the Swan River Valley hosted some fur trade competition when both the Hudson's Bay Company and the North West Company built fur trading posts along the river.

The broad agricultural valley — one of Manitoba's northernmost agricultural areas — received its first influx of settlers in 1898. The railway reached the Swan River area in the fall of 1899 and many more settlers followed. Within a couple of decades, efforts were underway to construct a highway between Dauphin and Swan River. Officially opened in 1923 "when a car from Swan River met a car from Dauphin," the highway "was a series of pot holes and washboard" for the first few years. Highway development kept pushing north, and by 1939, the highway reached The Pas.

Swan River Provincial Park, designated in 1974 and 0.02 square kilometres in size, is a wayside picnic area along Highway 10 just north of the community of Swan River. A classic highway rest stop, the park has picnic tables, lots of room for cars, and washrooms. The park is also on the banks of the Swan River. For a close up view of the river, a smaller picnic area just south of the park is set in the river bottom forest. The park also accommodates a government maintenance yard.

Swan River Provincial Park takes its name from the river and the community. Although the origin of the name is unconfirmed, black swans apparently used to inhabit the area.

If exploring Swan River's history interests you, visit the Swan River Historical Museum with many old buildings and displays across the highway and a little bit south from Swan River Provincial Park. Also check out the kettle stone at the Swan River Visitor Information Centre, unearthed during town excavations in 1966. ■

A classic highway rest stop, the park has picnic tables, washrooms and lots of room for cars.

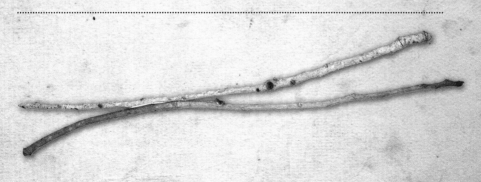

Trappist Monastery

APPARENTLY $50,000 was once offered by a Chicago firm for the secret of cheese making possessed by the Trappist monks at the monastery in St. Norbert. The monks who carried on their labours in silence did not share their secret.

The Trappists, monks of the Order of Cistercians of the Strict Observance, originated in France and moved to Quebec in the 1880s to escape religious persecution. In 1890 they were invited by Father Richot and Archbishop Tache to come to the Red River Settlement, a place where many French-Canadians were settling at the time (see St. Norbert Provincial Park for more information).

The monastery in St. Norbert along the La Salle River began with five members. Formally blessed in 1892, it "stood conspicuous on a hill surrounded by oak trees." In time, it supported 30 to 45 monks. The monks rose before dawn to participate in religious exercises and carried out various agricultural and other labours during the day. They took a vow of absolute silence, with the exception of certain

TRAPPIST
MONASTER
MONASTÈRE
DES TRAPPIST

AUGUST
AOÛT
1986

*Fire gutted the now vacant church
and residential wing in 1983.*

members who could converse with guests. Male visitors were invited to tour the monastery and the grounds, except between the hours of 11:30 a.m. and 2:00 p.m. In the early days, women were not welcome on the site.

While the monks were vegetarians, the kept livestock to sell in order to obtain the goods they could not produce themselves. They became famous for their honey and cheese. The monastery was self-sufficient. Urban encroachment, though, eventually made it more difficult for the monks to continue their lives of solitude, and in 1978, they moved to Holland, Manitoba. Fire gutted the now vacant church and residential wing in 1983.

In the 1990s, a guest house built on the site in 1912 was rehabilitated and is now occupied by the St. Norbert Arts Centre. A 0.02 square kilometre area including the limestone monastery ruins became a provincial heritage park in 2002.

Trappist Monastery is located two kilometres off Highway 75 in St. Norbert on Rue des Ruines du Monastere off Rue des Trappistes. ■

Turtle Mountain

LA VERENDRYE CALLED THIS LOVELY PART OF Manitoba the "blue jewel of the plains" when he first saw the area in 1738. For others, seeing the rise of Turtle Mountain from a distance creates a sense of anticipation and a feeling of curiosity. Turtle Mountain is part of an undulating semi-circular upland area that rises about 250 metres above surrounding land. The area is home to marshes, lakes, and deciduous forest. The hilly area may have been named because its general shape resembles a turtle. And as many visitors have observed, turtles are a common sight in the area's numerous lakes and marshes.

As the first dry land to appear after the retreat of the last glacier, it is also the oldest inhabited part of the province. The earliest evidence of habitation comes from a few isolated Clovis spear points from about 11,000 to 11,500 years ago found at various places in southwest Manitoba. The Clovis people would have entered Manitoba from the south or west when most of the province would have been covered by ice or Lake Agassiz.

Turtle Mountain was one of the first forest reserves established by the federal government in Manitoba in 1895, along with Spruce Woods and Riding Mountain. Forest reserves were also used for purposes other than forestry, and Turtle Mountain was used for hay production and livestock grazing. Wildfires regularly swept across the land and fireguards were ploughed throughout the reserve to help stop the spread of fires. These fireguards eventually became winding access roads that are still used today.

Turtle Mountain quickly became a recreational favourite for residents of southern Manitoba. By the time the provincial government assumed responsibility for its natural resources in 1930, Max Lake at Turtle Mountain was home to a well-attended campground. By the mid-1930s, lots were surveyed. The International Peace Garden, officially dedicated in 1932, was part of the Turtle Mountain Forest Reserve. The garden celebrates the long, undefended border between Canada and the United States.

Turtle Mountain became a provincial park in 1961 with an area of 186 square kilometres. Campgrounds with about 130 basic, electrical and electrical/water campsites are located at Adam and Max Lakes. Seasonal campsites are also available. An off-road James Lake cabin is available for use by hikers, skiers, and canoeists. The park also accommodates 40 cottages at Bower and Max Lakes.

To understand the natural forces at play in Turtle Mountain, including drought and forest succession, walk the Disappearing Lakes trail near Oskar Lake. The main source of water for lakes and marshes is precipitation in the form of rain and snow. During the drought of the 1930s, most of the lakes in Turtle Mountain were dry. Because of their shallowness and low oxygen levels, most Turtle Mountain lakes are not suitable for fish populations, although some lakes in the park are occasionally stocked for anglers.

Turtle Mountain is a great place to get out and about on foot. The Adam Lake trails start at the campground and give hikers several distance options from a few to 15 kilometres. To explore what lives in the park, walk the 1.6 kilometre descriptively named Wildlife trail with a viewing tower near Adam Lake. Moose, deer, beaver, turtles — the park is a haven for a variety of creatures. For some solitude, walk the two-kilometre Oskar Lake trail.

The park also contains trails for horseback riders and cyclists. An almost 20-kilometre canoe route connects Max Lake with Oskar Lake, traversing several lakes in between. If you are seeking a place for winter activities, Turtle Mountain has cross-country ski and snowmobile trails.

The east and most popular part of Turtle Mountain can be reached via Highway 10 about 14 kilometres south of Boissevain. The north part of the park is accessible from a gravel road from Highway 3. There is also a gravel access road on the west side of the park from Provincial Road 450. ▪

Twin Lakes

THE AREA BETWEEN CRANBERRY PORTAGE and Flin Flon was surveyed in 1945 to determine the best route for Highway 10. It was recommended that the road pass Otter Creek, Twin Lakes, Payuk Lake, Neso Lake, Athapapuskow Lake, Bakers Narrows, and Schist Lake. The highway was completed in 1950 and in that same year, a Northern Recreation Area dubbed "a vast scenic area containing some of the most beautiful inland lakes and other waterways in Canada," with "unsurpassed outdoor recreation pursuits such as fishing, camping, canoe and float plane travel, hunting, nature and geological studies" was created.

As with Neso Lake, Twin Lakes was part of this recreational area approximately 29 kilometres by 48 kilometres in size between Cranberry Portage and Flin Flon. By the end of the 1950s, the area included over 500 cottages with another 150 lots available for lease, and 16 tourist camps. Numerous roads were constructed from Highway 10 to cottage subdivisions and parking grounds on lakeshores. A recreational area was established at Twin Lakes in 1958, and in 1974 it became a provincial park at 0.01 square kilometres in size. Facilities in the park include a boat launch and a picnic area set among tall spruce trees. Cottages are located on Twin Lakes outside of the park. Twin Lakes, as its plural name suggests, appears to be two parallel lakes, both long and narrow, connected by a channel at their southwestern tips. The park is near this point.

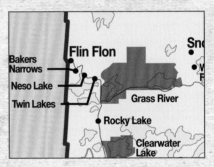

Like Grass River Provincial Park, Twin Lakes' neighbour to the east, the park's area spans the boundary between the Precambrian Shield and the Manitoba Lowlands. Cranberry Portage, named for the historic portage on the upper track fur trade route to Cumberland House and located just south of Twin Lakes, is considered to be a point where rivers either flow northeast to the Nelson River, or south to the Saskatchewan River. And despite the focus on recreation, the entire area retains a feel of wilderness, where the howl of a gray wolf may be as common as the cry of a loon, and the sight of a bald eagle, a bear or a moose is not unusual.

Twin Lakes is accessible via Provincial Road 635 from Highway 10, about 11 kilometres south of Bakers Narrows and about 14 kilometres north of Cranberry Portage. ∎

Wallace Lake

MANITOBA'S GOLD RUSH BEGAN IN 1911 when gold and other minerals were discovered near the community of Bissett in the Wanipigow River watershed. While not quite as famous as the Klondike gold rush of the late 1890s, prospectors still arrived in droves and claims were staked throughout the area. By 1927, silver and galena had been found near Wallace Lake east of Bissett, and over 80 claims had been staked in the area. To commemorate its mineral heritage, Wallace Lake itself is named after Dr. Robert C. Wallace, appointed first lecturer in Geology and Mineralogy at the University of Manitoba in 1910. The Wallace Building at the university, home to the Department of Geological Sciences, is also named after Dr. Wallace.

The southwestern shore of Wallace Lake has long been a recreational area. By the mid-1950s the province developed a campground, boat launch, and other facilities at Wallace Lake. The province began leasing cottage lots along the lake in 1959, but cottages had been established by miners and other locals years earlier.

Wallace Lake became a provincial park in 1961. It is one of those parks that appears somewhat remote on a map, yet is surprisingly busy on any given summer day. The 0.24 square-kilometre park includes a picnic area, small beach, boat launch, and a privately operated campground. The park also accommodates over 40 cottages and additional cottages are located outside of the park's boundaries. Popular with anglers, the lake is home to perch, northern pike, and tullibee.

The Wanipigow River with its headwaters in Ontario passes

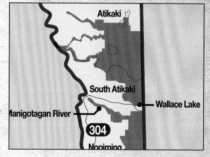

through Wallace Lake on its way to Lake Winnipeg. Canoeists can access the Wanipigow River canoe route from Wallace Lake Provincial Park. The park is also an important access point to nearby South Atikaki and Atikaki Provincial Parks. The Atikaki parks are not road-accessible, so if flying into the parks does not suit your budget, your best bet is to canoe in from Wallace Lake.

Wallace Lake Provincial Park is located approximately 17 miles east of Bissett just off Provincial Road 304. It is located just north of Nopiming Provincial Park. ∎

Watchorn

LAKE MANITOBA, THE PROVINCE'S THIRD largest lake, has five provincial "beach" parks along its shores — Lundar Beach, Manipogo, Margaret Bruce, St. Ambroise, and Watchorn. Watchorn Provincial Park on the east side of Lake Manitoba at Watchorn Bay boasts one of the larger sandy beaches although the sand is liberally scattered with small limestone rocks, evidence of the prevalence of limestone in the area. Just north of Watchorn is the community of Steep Rock, famous for its limestone cliffs. Small islets off shore can be seen from Watchorn Beach.

Settlers in the late nineteenth and early twentieth centuries travelled on the Fairford Trail, a trail that stretched between Oak Point and Fairford, often following the Lake Manitoba shoreline, but seldom in a straight line. Until the arrival of the railway, the trail was the only route into this part of the Interlake. The northern part of the trail was wooded with many sloughs, and settlers on the trail would sometimes travel "12 miles to actually gain one." Stopping places along the way provided food and beds on the floor for 25 cents, and those who could not afford the fee slept on the trail. Packed hard by countless feet of settlers, horses and oxen, parts of the trail that have not been cultivated for crops still remain visible today. Remnants of the trail can be seen in Watchorn Provincial Park.

In addition to the Fairford Trail and a good-sized beach, Watchorn Provincial Park offers 47 basic and electrical campsites, seasonal campsites, a group use area, and a picnic

area. A boat launch near the picnic area along Watchorn Creek provides a protected spot to launch before heading out on the lake.

Watchorn Bay, the creek, and the park take their names from H.T.D. Watchorn, a local postmaster who arrived in the area in 1903 and settled near the lake.

Watchorn Provincial Park is located 8 kilometres west of the community of Moosehorn on Provincial Road 237. Moosehorn is along Highway 6 between Ashern and Grahamdale, about 180 kilometres northwest of Winnipeg. ∎

**SWIMMING IS
UNSUPERVISED**

You are responsible.
Watch your children.
Know your own limits.
Drowning is preventable.
Inflatables are dangerous
in windy conditions.

BEACH RULES

No disruptive behaviour.
No alcoholic beverages.
No dogs allowed on beach.

911

300 m

Watchorn

Wekusko Falls

THERE IS SOMETHING UTTERLY CHARMING about Wekusko Falls Provincial Park. If there were an award for the prettiest provincial park in Manitoba, Wekusko Falls would be in the running. While Grass River Provincial Park, Wekusko's neighbour to the west, includes vast tracts of wilderness, Weskuko is small and picturesque. Perhaps it is the park's relatively small size of 0.88 square kilometres, the waterfall and rapids, its suspension bridges, or the nicely maintained campground and beach.

When the campground quiets for the night, listen to the sound of the Grass River as it tumbles over and through the falls and rapids.

Although not as high as Pisew Falls farther downstream, at Wekusko Falls, the Grass River drops 12 metres over a series of falls and rapids before entering Wekusko Lake. Not one, but two suspension bridges, take visitors over the falls and rapids. Initially constructed in August 1965 by men from the Royal Canadian Engineers, the bridges were officially handed over to the province in a hillside celebration that involved a blow-torch cutting a steel rod, rather than a more traditional ribbon cutting ceremony. Designated a provincial park in 1974, the area had been a recreation destination since Snow Lake to the north became a mining community in the mid 1940s. As with many other mining areas, gold was first discovered on the east shores of Wekusko Lake in 1913 and the area became home to several mine sites.

At Wekusko Falls, the Grass River occupies centre stage, and the park is situated on both sides of the river. Walking trails connect the campground to the day use area in a loop via the suspension bridges. When the campground with over

80 basic and electrical campsites quiets for the night, listen to the sound of the river as it tumbles over and through the falls and rapids on its way to entering Wekusko Lake. The park also has a boat launch.

Although not in Wekusko Falls Provincial Park, paddlers or boaters travelling upstream to Tramping Lake can see one of the province's largest collections of ancient pictographs, or rock paintings, created 1,500 to 3,000 years ago.

To get to Wekusko Falls, take Highway 392 (the highway to Snow Lake), north of Highway 39 just east of Grass River Provincial Park. ■

Wekusko Falls

Whitefish Lake

NAMED FOR THE PRODUCTIVE POPULATION OF WHITEFISH it once supported, Whitefish Lake is one of three provincial parks located within the Porcupine Provincial Forest (see also Bell Lake and North Steeprock Lake). Even in the 1940s, the lake was described as "a deep centrical lake of great beauty and one very dear to an angler's heart." Visitors gazing over the water at the hilly topography across the lake will be reminded that they are in the Porcupine Hills, part of the Manitoba Escarpment and one of the highest areas in the province.

If you have not visited Whitefish Lake Provincial Park, you will be pleasantly surprised when you do visit. About 23 kilometres from the community of Bowsman, or about 40 kilometres from Swan River, Whitefish Lake is an accessible park that feels like it is off the beaten path. Perhaps it is the short stretch of gravel road that one must travel to reach the park, or the fact that the park is situated in the Porcupine Provincial Forest very near the Saskatchewan border, that creates the expectation that few visitors will be at Whitefish Lake. But on any given summer day the bustle of activity will be noticeable upon arrival.

The park's 0.25 square kilometre area includes a popular campground with 40 basic campsites, a large day-use area with a picnic shelter, and a playground. A long narrow beach stretches along the shore of Whitefish Lake. A channel from the lake partly wraps around the campground providing a perfectly protected spot for boat launching. Anglers may hook whitefish,

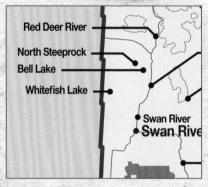

northern pike, perch, and walleye. Also along the channel, a boardwalk area with benches provides incentive to stop and take in the view.

The Porcupine Hills Forest Reserve was established in 1906, and like other forest reserves, its recreational potential was recognized. Development of the recreation area at Whitefish Lake began in 1963, and the area was designated a provincial park in 1974.

To get to Whitefish Lake Provincial Park, take Provincial Road 279 from the community of Bowsman, just north of Swan River along Highway 10. ■

Whitefish Lake

Whitemouth Falls

WHITEMOUTH FALLS PROVINCIAL PARK APPEARS TO BE TWO completely separate parks brought together under one name. The park, with a total area of 4.83 square kilometres, surrounds the confluence of the Whitemouth and Winnipeg Rivers in the vicinity of the Seven Sisters Generating Station.

Many people may be familiar with Whitemouth Falls wayside park, accessible from Provincial Road 307 in the community of Seven Sisters. This portion of the park, adjacent to Whitemouth Falls, has picnic facilities with barbeque pits. A popular spot for fishing, the falls are also a favourite site to view flocks of white pelicans. It is also worth stopping along the access road to the park for the best view of the Seven Sisters Generating Station, the largest dam on the Winnipeg River, which began operating in 1931. Benches near the roadside are well placed for leisurely viewing of the dam.

Whitemouth Falls was designated a provincial park in 1974, but the park has been a favourite recreation spot since dam construction. Even in the early 1930s, the park was billed as "a neat little summer resort at the mouth of the river." Going even

further back, archaeological evidence from three sites near the falls indicate that the area was a camping spot 4,800 years ago. The wayside picnic area portion is currently leased to the Rural Municipality of Whitemouth.

In 2007, Whitemouth Falls Provincial Park was expanded to include areas on the opposite side of the Winnipeg River along Provincial Road 211 between Pinawa Provincial Park and the town of Pinawa. This area was specifically designated to conserve Great Gray Owl habitat, and is considered to be one of the best places in the province to view Manitoba's provincial bird, especially in winter. The owls, with wingspans of 1.5 metres, can often be seen hunting for food along the edges of meadows and roadsides. In summer, the owls retreat deeper into the forest and are seen less often.

Whitemouth Falls Provincial Park is one of three provincial parks along the Winnipeg River — see also Pinawa and Whiteshell. ∎

Even in the early 1930s the park was billed as a neat little summer resort at the mouth of the river.

Whiteshell

WHAT IS NOT TO LOVE ABOUT THE WHITESHELL? It has been called many things over the years. Land of crystal lakes and age-old granite, happy holiday-land for campers, a pine-scented natural playground, a place where the north comes down to meet you, and many, many other things. Or as the Parks Guide states, "You could spend years exploring Whiteshell Provincial Park and still not experience it all." All true. The irresistible beauty of rock and water keeps many people returning year after year.

For an estimated 8,000 years people have been visiting the Whiteshell, first believed to be inhabited by an Algonquin-speaking people, ancestors of the Ojibway. Petroforms or rock "alignments" in the form of snakes, turtles, humans, and other shapes occur throughout the area. Set in the Precambrian Shield physiographic region, the Whiteshell is believed to be named after the small white cowrie or megis shell found in the area.

Explorers and fur traders first visited the Whiteshell in the 1730s, and the Winnipeg River which forms the Whiteshell's northern boundary became part of the main water transportation route from the east. The river, known as "the grandest and most beautiful river," was also known for its challenging falls and rapids along its length. The old portage route past Sturgeon Falls is still visible, and still used by recreational paddlers today. At times, the Whiteshell River was used as an alternate route.

The river's importance as a transportation route was lessened with the coming of the railway. The

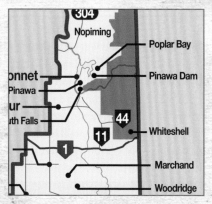

Canadian Pacific Railway between Winnipeg and Thunder Bay first became operational in 1883. The Canadian National Railway built a line in the vicinity just over 20 years later. Railway employees and travellers were the first to glimpse the recreational potential of the Whiteshell.

Prior to 1930, natural resources were the responsibility of the federal government, and in the 1920s the federal government leased cottage lots in the areas around Brereton, Nora, Florence, West Hawk and Falcon Lakes. Access to the lots was via railway. After the transfer of natural resources to Manitoba in 1930, the province established the Whiteshell Forest Reserve.

Hard labour for the development of cottage subdivisions and recreational facilities was readily available during the Great Depression in the dirty thirties, and relief camps were established in the Whiteshell Forest Reserve, employing up to 350 men. This make-work project began constructing roads near Falcon Lake and Brereton, a ranger station, dock and lookout tower at West Hawk, and installed a telephone line to West Hawk. By the mid-1930s, cottages were well-established. In 1932 the Trans-Canada Highway between Winnipeg and Kenora was completed. The highway (now called Highway 44) took drivers from Lockport through Garson, Beausejour, and

A pedestrian bridge by the Nutimik Lake campground spans the Whiteshell River near Sturgeon Falls.

Whiteshell

Whiteshell

Whitemouth, to Rennie, and through the Whiteshell and into Ontario. By 1938, black-topping of the Trans-Canada Highway through the forest reserve induced even more visitors to the area and development hit its stride. By the mid 1950s, the Falcon Lake townsite was taking shape, and work began on the golf course in 1956.

The very first illustrated promotional booklet extolling the virtues of the Whiteshell with photographs and five colour reproductions of water colour paintings by Walter J. Philips was issued in 1940, and the Whiteshell was fast becoming a favourite topic in local newspapers. In 1940, the *Winnipeg Tribune* reported that the forest reserve's "crystal clear water cooled by a natural fan belt of fir, spruce, and pine persuades the vacationist to extend his stay, secure in the fastness of the primeval forest." The Whiteshell also took centre stage in other promotional brochures published throughout the 1940s and '50s by the province's Tourist Bureau. Visitors needed little enticement and responded in droves. By the 1950s, campgrounds and beaches were filled to overflowing.

Government development in the Whiteshell and other areas of the province was a primary impetus for official park establishment. The provincial government was expending much time and money on recreation development, and wanted to consolidate planning and management of such expenditures. The first Pro-

vincial Parks Act was proclaimed in 1960, and the Whiteshell, along with Duck Mountain, Turtle Mountain, Grand Beach, became our first large provincial parks in 1961.

Of the three large Canadian Shield parks along the Ontario border (see also Nopiming and Atikaki) the Whiteshell at 2,721 square kilometres in size is the most developed of the three. That said, there is still ample opportunity to enjoy the natural beauty of the area, both in proximity to recreational developments, and in backcountry areas much more off the beaten path. Sightings of deer, red foxes, black bears, and other wild creatures, are common. And watch for beavers and river otters in the area's creeks and rivers.

Development in the Whiteshell generally falls into three main areas centred around Falcon, West Hawk, and Caddy Lakes in the south, the centre area from Rennie along Provincial Roads 307 and 309 to lakes such as White, Big Whiteshell, Nutimik, Dorothy, and others, and the north part, around Pointe du Bois.

It is in the south and central parts of the park that you will find its 11 main campgrounds with over 900 campsites at Betula, Big Whiteshell, Brereton, Caddy, Falcon Beach, Falcon Lakeshore, Nutimik, Opapiskaw, Otter Falls, West Hawk, and White Lake. At Nutimik you will also find yurts, and many campgrounds also have seasonal campsites. There are also a couple of campgrounds near Pointe du Bois. Most campgrounds

Petroforms or rock alignments in the form of snakes, turtles, humans, and other shapes occur throughout the area.

Whiteshell

Whiteshell

are located near some of the park's most popular beaches. If camping is not your preference, the park is home to several privately operated lodges and resorts. Or you just may have, or know someone with, a cottage in the park since the Whiteshell is home to over 3,300 cottages, the most cottages in any provincial park. For many who enjoy sleeping in their own beds, the Whiteshell is also the perfect day trip due to its proximity to Winnipeg and other communities in eastern Manitoba.

The scenic Whiteshell is ideally suited to walking, offering both easy and challenging hikes, and everything in between. Try the Pine Point Rapids trail for an easy walk with great views at the farthest point. A five-kilometre loop takes walkers to the Pine Point Rapids on the Whiteshell River. If you have energy for a longer walk, try an extra three-kilometre loop that will let you follow the Whiteshell River further downstream as it passes through Acorn and Viburnum Falls. For a beautifully challenging hike, try the Hunt Lake trail that follows the shores of Hunt Lake and West Hawk. It is an out-and-back trail with both blissful views and steep rock faces

Winter is no excuse to stop visiting the Whiteshell.

to climb. McGillivray Falls offers walkers an almost three-kilometre loop or a longer 4.6-kilometre trail to McGillvray Lake. The Centennial trail, maintained by Boy Scouts, takes walkers in the opposite direction from McGillivray Falls. Marked with stone cairns, this gorgeous trail leads walkers on high granite cliffs among the treetops.

At over 60 kilometres in length, the Mantario trail in the back-country between Caddy Lake and Big Whiteshell Lake offers some of the most challenging hiking in the park, but also some of the greatest scenic rewards. The entire trail may take several days to walk, or portions can be done as day hikes.

There are many more walking trails in the park, including the Whiteshell River, Amisk, Jessica Lake, Falcon Creek, Forester's Footsteps near Betula Lake, and others. A newly constructed bridge over the Whiteshell River near its confluence with the Winnipeg takes walkers from the campground at Nutimik Lake to Sturgeon Falls. The Trans Canada Trail also traverses the park. A park map or a walking guide will help you find the right trail.

Paddlers have just as much choice as walkers. For a multi-day paddle, canoeists can reach the historic Winnipeg River that forms the Whiteshell's northern boundary from Big Whiteshell and Crowduck Lakes. Or if a shorter paddle is of interest, the Winnipeg River can also be accessed at Pointe du Bois or from Nutimik, Dorothy, or Eleanor Lakes. The 85-kilometre Whiteshell River canoe route takes paddlers from Caddy Lake to Betula Lake. If a two or three day paddle down the Whiteshell River is not possible, then be sure to try a day trip from Caddy

Whiteshell

Lake through a tunnel below the railway into South Cross Lake, and return. Any lake in the Whiteshell will welcome a canoe or kayak for an afternoon paddle. Find a boat launch and enjoy.

Beyond the incredible selection of camping sites, walking trails, beaches and boating opportunities, the Whiteshell has several unique points of interest.

The Alfred Hole Goose Sanctuary, named after an outdoorsman and mink rancher who lived near Rennie, began unintentionally when Alf received four Canada goose goslings in the spring of 1939. Hand-raised, they mingled with Alf's chickens. The nearby Rennie River was dammed to form a goose pond. Over the years, geese bred, migrated, and returned each year. The sanctuary is a popular stop for migrating geese each spring and fall, plus many geese choose to spend the summer. A 2.5 kilometre interpretive trail extends from the interpretive centre part way around the goose pond. The Whiteshell Trappers Museum, a replica of a trappers cabin, is on the grounds of the goose sanctuary.

Whiteshell Natural History Museum is located along Provincial Road 307 at Nutimik Lake. This charming old log building with creaky floors is chock full of stuffed wildlife and displays about everything you wanted to know about the natural and cultural history of the Whiteshell, including information about the local wild rice harvest, the Bannock Point Petroforms, and many other things.

West Hawk Lake is perhaps the most famous meteor crater lake in Manitoba. It is believed that a

Any lake in the Whiteshell will welcome a canoeist or kayaker for a paddle.

meteorite hit the earth about 100 million years ago, creating a crater 2.4 kilometres in diameter. At 111 metres deep, the lake is the deepest in Manitoba making it a popular dive site for scuba divers. The West Hawk Museum with displays about the area's geological history is located by the West Hawk campground office.

The Whiteshell Fish Hatchery has been a fixture in the park since 1942. Fishing has always been one of the main attractions in the Whiteshell, and the hatchery has helped to maintain fish populations. In 2001, an interpretive centre developed jointly between the province and Fish Futures was opened. Hatchery tours are available in the summer.

Winter is no excuse to stop visiting the Whiteshell. All main roads are ploughed and maintained, many resorts are open all-season, and there is lots to keep everyone busy and warm. Try downhill skiing at Falcon Ridge, sleigh rides at Falcon Beach, ice fishing, snowshoeing, cross-country skiing, and snowmobiling. Walking, too. And do not forget to pack a camera. Many rapids and falls flow through the winter, creating eye-catching ice-sculpted landscapes.

With so much to do and see in the Whiteshell, it is easy to forget that one of the most enjoyable things to do is to take a deep breath, relax and savour the moment. In the Whiteshell, that is do-able just about everywhere.

The Whiteshell is accessible from the Trans-Canada Highway, from Highway 44 (through Rennie), from Provincial Road 307 (through Seven Sisters), and from PR 313 (to get to Pointe du Bois). ■

William Lake

William Lake is part of the Turtle Mountain upland area dubbed "the blue jewel of the plains" by La Verendrye.

T HE TURTLE'S BACK TRAIL IS A POPULAR WALKING
TRAIL that begins in William Lake Provincial Park and
continues through the Turtle Mountain Community Pasture.
Walkers can stay on the trail that makes a complete circum-
navigation of the lake, or take a trail extension that leads to a
viewing tower at the highest point in the Turtle Mountain area.
If Turtle Mountain was named because the hilly area is in the
general shape of a turtle, then the highest point would indeed
be the turtle's back. From the tower, visitors are treated to
an amazing view of the surrounding area in all directions,
including the hills and forests, nearby farms and towns, and
the peace tower at the International Peace Garden.

William Lake

William Lake Provincial Park is
part of the Turtle Mountain upland
area, an area dubbed the "blue jewel
of the plains" by La Verendrye in
1738. The park is located just east of
Turtle Mountain Provincial Park and
just north of the U.S. border. William
Lake was part of the Turtle Mountain
Forest Reserve established by the
federal government in 1895 and used
for forestry, hay production, and
livestock grazing.

Like Turtle Mountain Provincial
Park, William Lake has long been a
popular recreation spot with local
residents. In the late 1880s there were
apparently five men named William
at a picnic along the lakeshore. The
lake became known as William Lake,
and the name stuck.

As with Turtle Mountain,
William Lake became a provincial
park in 1961. But unlike sprawling
Turtle Mountain, William Lake is
small and intimate at two square
kilometres in size. The campground

at William Lake has over 50 basic
sites along the lake's wooded
shoreline. The park also has picnic
sites, a beach, and a boat launch. As
the deepest and one of the largest
lakes in the Turtle Mountain area,
William Lake is often stocked with
brown trout for anglers. Due to its
depth, the lake also supports a native
population of walleye.

To get to William Lake, take
Highway 10 south of Boissevain to
Provincial Road 341, head east to PR
444, then head south to the park. ∎

Winnipeg Beach

MANICURED, MATURE, AND ESTABLISHED — all words that come to mind when trying to describe Winnipeg Beach. Not surprising really, as this Grand Dame of beaches has been a recreational destination for over a century. It was during the summer of 1900 that the Canadian Pacific Railway's Sir William Whyte cruised the west shore of Lake Winnipeg looking for a suitable spot to create a resort. He found it about 70 kilometres north of the city. The CPR no doubt named its resort Winnipeg Beach to attract Winnipeggers to their own beach playground. By the time the railway tracks reached Winnipeg Beach in 1903, a train station, dance pavilion, and community had been developed. Winnipeggers responded in droves, and the locale became known as simply "The Beach". No adjective required.

The first automobile reached Winnipeg Beach in 1913, although the trip took almost a day over rough trails. As roads improved and automobile use became more widespread, travel by rail saw a corresponding decrease. In 1961, the CPR ceased train service to the beach and in 1964, the amusement park closed. For economic development purposes, the province acquired some of the CPR property, and Winnipeg Beach Provincial Park was designated in 1968.

Stretching along the western shore of Lake Winnipeg in the town of Winnipeg Beach, Winnipeg Beach Provincial Park surrounds the community's downtown area to the north, east, and south, covering approximately 0.4 square kilometres in total.

The large grassy portion of the park extending north of the town's

centre toward the marina has numerous picnic sites and a playground. Lots of mature trees provide much needed shade in the summertime. This area is home to "Anishinaabe," a red cedar carving almost eleven metres high that honours the Ojibway, Assiniboine and Cree of Manitoba. Carved by Peter Toth in 1991, the statue is part of the whispering giant series that he began carving in the early 1970s.

The centre portion of the park is located between the town's centre and the lake. Sip a latte while strolling the boardwalk along the lake, or visit one of the many restaurants and stores in the town of Winnipeg Beach. Many of these amenities are open year round. A bandstand is often the focal point for summer concerts and other events.

The south end of the park includes Manitoba's newest provincial park campground, with 120 serviced sites, making it the only provincial park campground set in a town. How civilized. Nearby is the 400-metre tall steel water tower built in 1928, the only CPR structure that remains and one of the most visible sights in Winnipeg Beach. The tower was designated a provincial heritage site in 1998.

To get to Winnipeg Beach Provincial Park, follow Highway 9 north of Winnipeg about 70 kilometres to the town of Winnipeg Beach, and watch for signage pointing to the park. Winnipeg Beach is one of eight provincial parks along the shores of Lake Winnipeg. See also Elk Island, Grand Beach, Patricia Beach, Camp Morton, Hnausa Beach, Hecla/ Grindstone, and Beaver Creek. ■

Woodridge

ON THE EDGE OF THE SANDILANDS PROVINCIAL FOREST in southeast Manitoba lies Woodridge Provincial Park, approximately one kilometre north of the community of Woodridge and about 50 kilometres southeast of Steinbach.

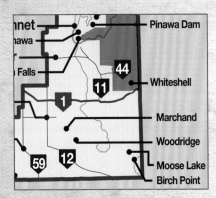

The railway reached Marchand in 1898 and Sprague in 1901, and Woodridge was located along the route between the two. The railway spurred growth of the forest industry in southeast Manitoba, and much of the Sandilands area was logged in the late nineteenth and early twentieth centuries. By 1923, the Sandilands Forest Reserve was created by the federal government.

The Sandilands area is aptly named. It is part of a series of sand and gravel end-moraine ridges deposited during the last period of glaciation that stretch from Victoria Beach through Milner Ridge and further south to the Sandilands area. The sandy soils support extensive jack pine forests.

Like nearby Marchand Provincial Park, Woodridge became a provincial park in 1974. While the park contains no park facilities other than a couple of picnic tables, it is used as a meeting place. The area around Woodridge is home to many all terrain vehicle and snowmobile trails. About half of the park's 0.01 square kilometre area is open field with room to park trucks and trailers. There is also an old fire look-out tower in the park that is no longer in use.

If unexplained mysteries interest you, then Woodridge just might pique your interest for reasons other than recreation. The mysterious "ghost" light of Woodridge has intrigued folks for decades. Described as an "intense white light, yellow-or-ange around the edges," the light has been observed on several occasions near Woodridge. In 1970, an observer reported to the *Winnipeg Free Press* that "the light appeared on the horizon for about five minutes, then faded and made five more brief appearances throughout the evening." In 2005, the *Free Press* explained that "it is said to appear tiny and faint initially, then increase in size and brilliance to the point that it becomes almost blinding. Apparently, it has even chased folks who have come to see it."

To get to Woodridge Provincial Park, travel Provincial Road 210 from the community of Ste. Anne, through La Broquerie and Marchand, to Woodridge. ∎

Yellow Quill

YELLOW QUILL WAS A SAULTEAUX BORN AROUND 1830, and in 1860, he became a chief. His band lived at Hamilton Crossing about 35 kilometres southwest of Portage la Prairie on land deeded to them by the government. They called their land "Indian Gardens." In 1876 during treaty negotiations, Chief Yellow Quill selected the Swan Lake Reserve for his band, but was unable to convince many of his people to follow him. They remained at Indian Gardens and were rejoined by Chief Yellow Quill. By the 1880s, however, settlers began occupying lands in the area, a situation that concerned the band greatly. It was not until 1913, after Chief Yellow Quill's death, that a reserve was established at Hamilton Crossing called Indian Gardens Reserve.

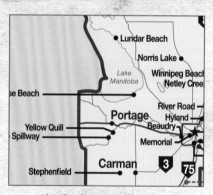

Chief Yellow Quill was well-respected by government agents during treaty negotiations, and has since been commemorated in many ways. A school in Portage la Prairie was named after the chief, as was the Yellowquill Trail. To celebrate Manitoba's 125th birthday in 1995, the *Winnipeg Free Press* published a list of 125 people who had an impact on the history and development of our province. Chief Yellow Quill made the list. In 1997, a small wayside park at the intersection of the Yellowquill Trail and the Trans-Canada Highway became Yellow Quill Provincial Park.

Yellow Quill is a triangular-shaped wayside park, 0.03 square kilometres in size, with picnic tables. The entire park appears as a slightly undulating grassy plain punctuated with natural poplar bluffs. It serves as a sunny highway rest stop and a park for the local community.

About half a kilometre south of the park along the Yellowquill Trail, you will see the Fort la Reine cairn, erected to mark the establishment of the fort by La Verendrye in 1738. Just further down the Yellowquill Trail, you will find Portage Spillway Provincial Park.

Yellow Quill Provincial Park is located along the Trans-Canada Highway at the junction of the highway and the Yellowquill Trail in Portage la Prairie. Access to the park is from a service road parallel to the highway. ■

Zed Lake

IT IS HARD NOT TO USE THE CLICHÉ, *last but not least,* while describing Zed Lake. Last alphabetically, the most northerly provincial park campground in Manitoba, and the farthest road-accessible provincial park for anyone living in southern Manitoba. But certainly not least.

Anyone camping on or near June 21 would notice almost 18 hours of sunlight, plus over an hour of twilight in both morning and evening, making for long days to enjoy the lake.

According to the Manitoba Geographical Names Program, Zed Lake is in fact a phonetic representation of the letter "z". Nearby are Ex Lake and Wye Lake, other alphabetically named lakes in the area.

Located 27 kilometres from the town of Lynn Lake — the self-proclaimed Sportfishing Capital of Manitoba — Zed Lake is probably best known to anglers who fish its cool, clean waters for lake trout, walleye and northern pike.

Although Zed Lake became a provincial park in 1961, it was first developed as a recreation spot with cottages, a beach, change rooms, and washrooms in the mid-1950s, not long after the mining community of Lynn Lake was established. Neely's Beach on Zed Lake was named after

Lynn Lake's first town administrator, Charles G. Neely, and officially dedicated on a September day in 1957 when "snow fell so hard at times that visibility was almost zero."

At Zed Lake Provincial Park, a small beach, boat launch and dock provide access to the lake. The park includes a small campground with ten basic campsites set in the sandy soils and Jack pine of the Churchill River upland area. At 56.91 degrees north in latitude, Manitoba's most northerly provincial park campground is almost in the land of the midnight sun. Anyone camping on or near June 21st will notice almost 18 hours of sunlight, plus over an hour of twilight in both morning and evening, making for some long days to enjoy the lake. The park's 0.12 square kilometre area also accommodates 25 cottages.

With the official opening of Provincial Road 391 connecting Thompson to Lynn Lake in 1974, the park became road-accessible to everyone. From Lynn Lake, take PR 394 to Zed Lake. If in the Lynn Lake area, also visit Zed Lake's sister park, Burge Lake Provincial Park. ∎

Zed Lake

Maps

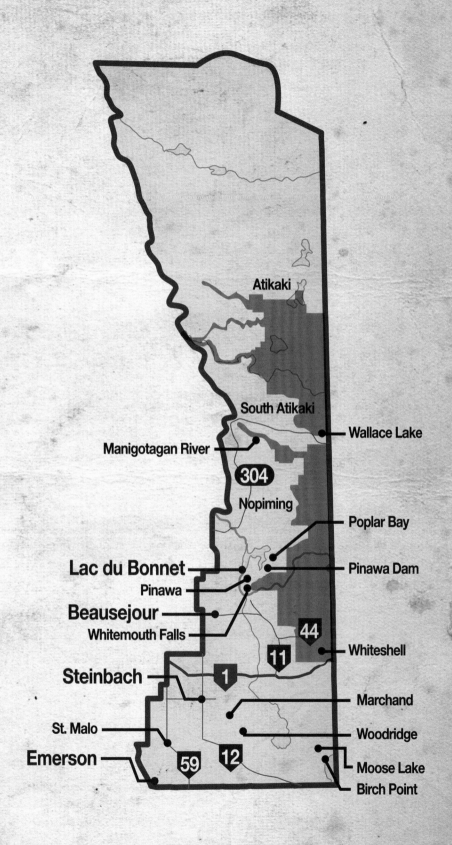

Atikaki

South Atikaki

Wallace Lake

Manigotagan River

304

Nopiming

Poplar Bay

Pinawa Dam

Lac du Bonnet

Pinawa

Beausejour

Whitemouth Falls

44

11

Whiteshell

Steinbach

1

Marchand

St. Malo

Woodridge

Emerson

59

12

Moose Lake

Birch Point

Maps

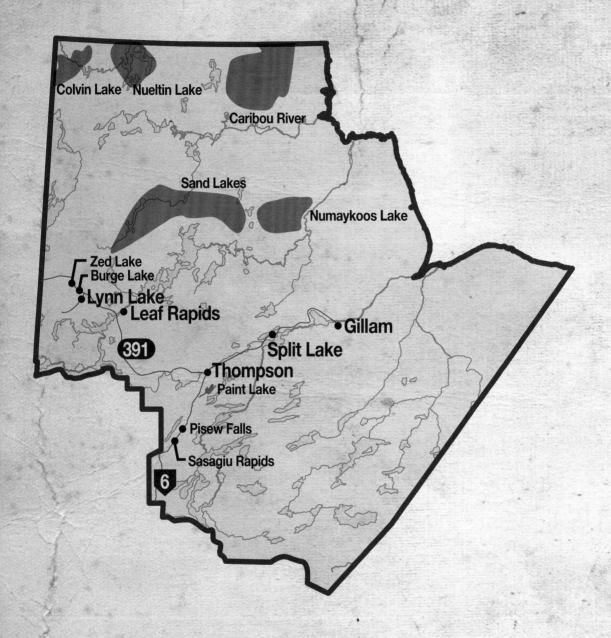

Colvin Lake   Nueltin Lake

Caribou River

Sand Lakes

Numaykoos Lake

Zed Lake
Burge Lake
Lynn Lake
Leaf Rapids

391

Gillam
Split Lake

Thompson
Paint Lake

Pisew Falls

Sasagiu Rapids

6

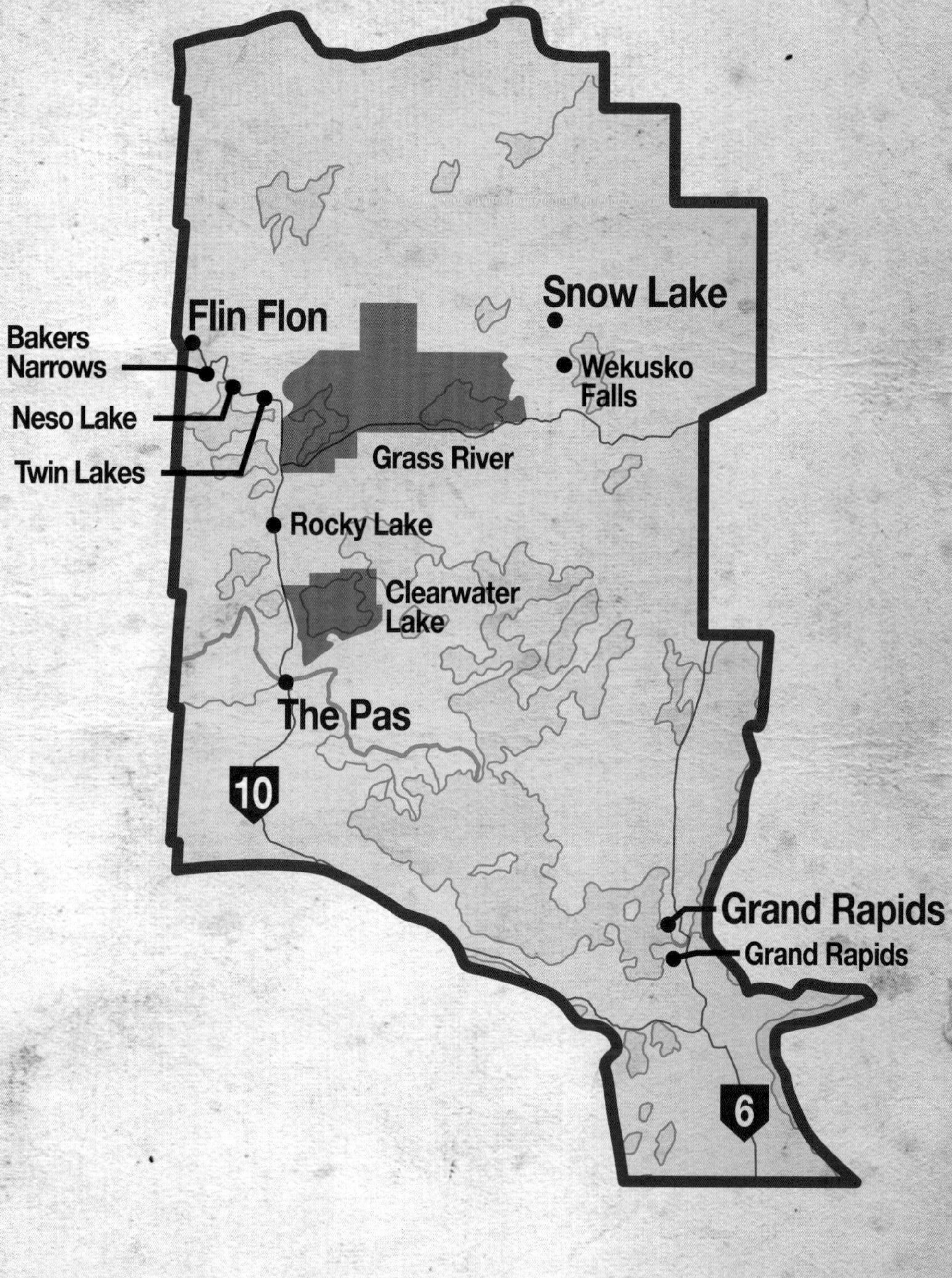

Bakers
Narrows

Neso Lake

Twin Lakes

Flin Flon

Snow Lake

Wekusko
Falls

Grass River

Rocky Lake

Clearwater
Lake

The Pas

10

Grand Rapids

Grand Rapids

6

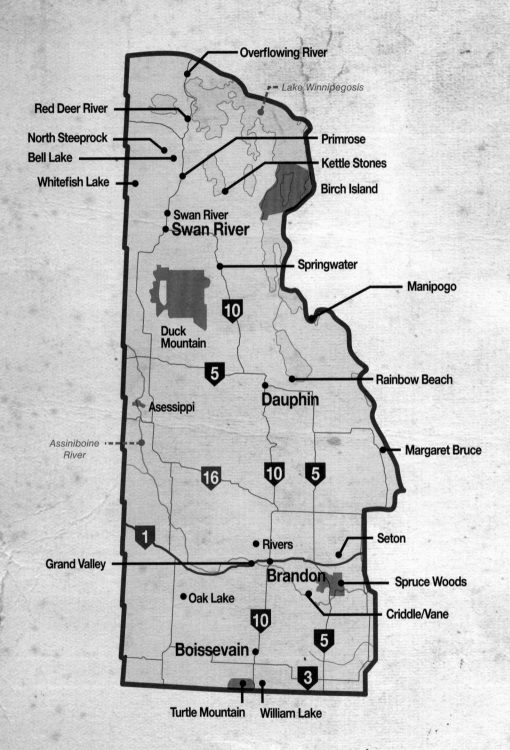

Overflowing River

Lake Winnipegosis

Red Deer River

North Steeprock

Bell Lake

Whitefish Lake

Primrose

Kettle Stones

Birch Island

Swan River

Swan River

Springwater

Manipogo

10

Duck
Mountain

5

Rainbow Beach

Asessippi

Dauphin

*Assiniboine
River*

Margaret Bruce

16   **10**   **5**

1

Rivers

Seton

Grand Valley

Brandon

Spruce Woods

•Oak Lake

Criddle/Vane

10

Boissevain

5

3

Turtle Mountain   William Lake

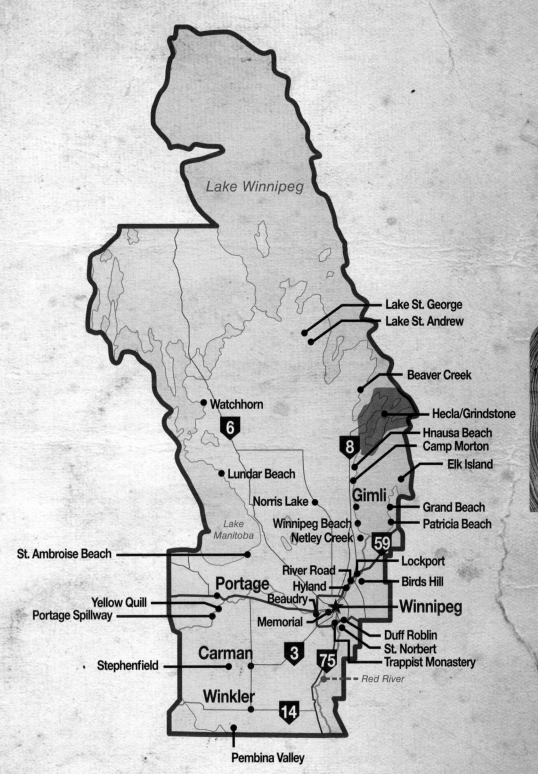

Lake Winnipeg

Lake St. George
Lake St. Andrew

Beaver Creek

Hecla/Grindstone

Hnausa Beach
Camp Morton
Elk Island

Watchhorn

6

Lundar Beach

Gimli

Grand Beach
Patricia Beach

Norris Lake

8

Lake
Manitoba

Winnipeg Beach
Netley Creek

59

St. Ambroise Beach

Lockport

River Road

Birds Hill

Portage

Hyland
Beaudry

Winnipeg

Yellow Quill
Portage Spillway

Memorial

Duff Roblin
St. Norbert
Trappist Monastery

Stephenfield

Carman

3

75

Winkler

Red River

14

Pembina Valley

Maps

Recommended Reading

If visiting Manitoba's provincial parks and places in between, consider the following guides that provide ideas for picnicking, walking, canoeing, and wildlife watching:

Canoeing Manitoba's River, by John Buchanan. Calgary: Rocky Mountain Books, 1997.

A Daytripper's Guide to Manitoba, by Bartley Kives. Winnipeg: Great Plains, updated edition 2010.

Hiking the Heartland: Explore Manitoba on Foot, by Prairie Pathfinders. Winnipeg, 2007

Manitoba, Naturally: Scenic Secrets of Manitoba, by Bill Stilwell. Winnipeg, 2006.

Manitoba Picnic Perfect, by Prairie Pathfinders. Winnipeg, 2003

Manitoba Wild: Scenic Secrets of Manitoba, by Bill Stilwell. Winnipeg, 2010.

Pelicans to Polar Bears: Watching Wildlife in Manitoba, by Catherine Senecal. Winnipeg: Heartland, revised edition, 2003.

Wilderness Rivers of Manitoba, by Hap Wilson. Erin, ON: Boston Mills Press, revised edition, 2004.

Winnipeg Walks, by Prairie Pathfinders. Winnipeg, 2004.

Selected Bibliography

Alonsa Manitoba Village History Committee. (1993). *Many trails to Manitou-Wapah.*

Badertscher, P.M. (1987). *Hill of the buffalo chase: 1982 excavations at the Stott site.* Winnipeg: Manitoba Department of Culture, Heritage and Recreation.

Bossenmaier, E.F. (1973, Autumn). *Clandeboye Bay.* Manitoba Nature, 10-15.

Bremner, B. (1985). *Provincial wayside review and systems plan.* Winnipeg: Manitoba Natural Resources.

Bryce, G. (1897, February). *The Lake of the Woods: its history, geology, mining and manufacturing.* MHS Transactions, 1(49).

Carberry History Committee. (1982). Carberry Plains - century one.

Carmichael, P.H. (1986). *Prehistory of the Turtle Mountain District: an initial sketch.* Winnipeg. Manitoba Department of Culture, Heritage and Recreation.

Cayford, J.H. (1959). *Seeding jack pine on the Sandilands Forest Reserve, Manitoba, 1925 to 1955.* Canada Department of Northern Affairs and National Resources.

Copen, S.J. (1975). *Preliminary report on Paint Lake Provincial Recreation Park and Pisew Falls Wayside interpretive plans.*

Criddle, A. (1973). *Criddle-de-Diddle-Ensis.*

Damas and Smith Limited. (1982). *River Road parkway: proposed project plan.*

Darland, R. (2000, Feb/Mar). *A man ahead of his time.* National Wildlife, 38(2), 43.

Downes, P.G. (1943). *Sleeping island: the story of one man's travels in the great barren lands of the Canadian north.* New York: Coward-McCann.

Edie, B. (2009, Fall). *Oak Lake.* The Cottager, 30.

Encyclopedia of Manitoba. (2007). Winnipeg: Great Plains.

Eyler, P. *Goldrush: on the trail of the quartz miners.* Manitoba Nature, 9-13.

Fur trade in the Swan River region. (1983). Winnipeg: Historic Resources Branch.

Geographical names of Manitoba. (2000). Winnipeg: Manitoba Conservation.

Gibbons, G. (1945). *Early Red River homes.* MHS Transactions, 3.

Hardship and happines: Manitoba local history of the Steep Rock, Hilbre, Faulkner, Grahamdale and surrounding areas. (1974). Steep Rock, Manitoba: Interlake Pioneers.

Hayward, W. (1944). *Investigation survey Duck Mountain Forest Reserve: descriptions of lakes.* Winnipeg: Manitoba Department of Mines and Natural Resources.

Hnausa History Book Committee. (2004). *Hnausa reflections: a history of the Breidavik district.*

Hoole, A.F. (1970). *Outdoor recreational use and potential of Lake Athapapuskow.* Department of Indian Affairs and Northern Development.

Huck, B. (2002). *Exploring the fur trade routes of North America.* Winnipeg: Heartland.

Johnson, K. (1979). *The boreal forest: an ecologist's view.* Manitoba Nature, 20(2), 14-23.

Jones, G.A. (1973). *Site analysis for recreational development on Rocky Lake.* The Pas: Manitoba Department of Mines, Resources, and Environmental Management.

Lemoine. S. (1978). *Grand Beach: the grand old days.* Winnipeg: Manitoba Department of Tourism, Recreation, and Cultural Affairs.

MacCharles, S. (1983). *Natural history themes: Beaudry Provincial Park.* Winnipeg: Manitoba Natural Resources.

MacDonald, J. (Ed.). (2000). *The lake: an illustrated history of Manitobans' cottage country.* Winnipeg: Great Plains.

Manitoba, Canada: inside the rim of adventure. Department of Mines and Natural Resources.

Manitoba Conservation. (2008). *Atikaki Provincial Park and Bloodvein Canadian Heritage River management plan.*

Manitoba Conservation. (2002). *Grand Beach Provincial Park management plan.*

Manitoba Conservation. (2010). *Manitoba parks guide: life's great outdoors in Manitoba's provincial parks.*

Manitoba Conservation. *System plan for Manitoba's provincial parks.*

Manitoba Department of Cultural Affairs and Historical Resources. (1983). *St. Norbert Heritage Park.*

Manitoba Department of Mines, Resources, and Environmental Management. (1973). *Grand Rapids area present recreational development and potential.*

Manitoba Department of Mines, Resources, and Environmental Management. (1982). *Interim management guidelines for Nopiming Provincial Park.*

Manitoba Department of Mines, Resources, and Environmental Management. (1975). *St. Malo reservoir recreation potential study.*

Manitoba Department of Tourism and Recreation. *Development Plan for Moose Lake area.*

Manitoba Department of Tourism and Recreation. (1969). *Evaluation of Grand Rapids recreation developments: October 21st, 1969.*

Manitoba Department of Tourism and Recreation. *Proposed Elk Island heritage area.*

Manitoba Department of Tourism, Recreation, and Cultural Affairs. *Investment opportunity guidelines: a resort at Sasagiu Rapids, Manitoba.*

Manitoba Department of Tourism, Recreation, and Cultural Affairs. (1972). *Lake Dauphin: effect of water levels on recreation.*

Manitoba Department of Tourism, Recreation, and Cultural Affairs. (1976). *The parks of Manitoba.*

Manitoba Department of Urban Development and Municipal Affairs. (1970). *Report on Stephenfield Reservoir recreational development.*

Manitoba Natural Resources. *Asessippi Provincial Park master plan.*

Manitoba Natural Resources. (1984). *Grass River Provincial Park management plan.*

Manitoba Natural Resources. (1988). *Hecla Grindstone Provincial Park management plan.*

Manitoba Natural Resources. (1986). *Interim guidelines for Clearwater Lake Provincial Park.*

Manitoba Natural Resources. (1983). *Interim management guidelines: Beaudry Provincial Park.*

Manitoba Natural Resources. (1985). *Proposal for redevelopment of Winnipeg Beach Provincial Recreation Park.*

Manitoba Natural Resources. (1985). *Turtle Mountain Provincial Park: management plan.*

Manitoba Natural Resources. (1983). *Whiteshell master plan.*

Manitoba's Romantic Northland. (1948). *Manitoba Travel and Publicity Bureau.*

Mazur, D.H. (1975). Outdoor recreation master plan Manigotagan-Bissett region. *Winnipeg: Manitoba Department of Tourism, Recreation and Cultural Affairs.*

Bibliography

McDougall, B. (2001, March/April). *Manitoba's old salt.* Canadian Geographic, 121(2), 23.

McMahon, B. & Koonz, W. (1991). *Abundance and reproductive success of colonial waterbirds on Lake Winnipegosis, 1987-1989.* Winnipeg: Manitoba Natural Resources.

McTavish, W.B. (1950). *A biological investigation of Mistik River chain of lakes Payuk, Neso and Nisto.* Winnipeg: Manitoba Department of Mines and Natural Resources.

McTavish, W.B. (1954). *A biological survey of Wallace Lake.* Winnipeg: Manitoba Department of Mines and Natural Resources.

Merkl, A. (1982). *Heritage park proposal and development scheme for the Pinawa Power Dam.*

Mullaney, R. (1981). *A history of Birch River and districts.*

Nicholson, G.C. (1964). *The Grass River canoe route.*

Prehistory of the Lockport site. (1985). Winnipeg: Manitoba Culture, Heritage and Recreation.

Red River salt makers. (1963, January). Manitoba Pageant.

Report on measures for the control of the waters of Lakes Winnipeg and Manitoba. (1958). Winnipeg: Lakes Winnipeg and Manitoba Board.

River Road: an overview report: a scenic historic route. (1973).

Rounds, R.C. (1990). *A user needs survey of Rivers Provincial Recreation Park, Manitoba.* Brandon: Brandon University.

Russell, F. Mistehay *Sakahegan, the great lake: the beauty and the treachery of Lake Winnipeg.* Winnipeg: Heartland.

Saurette, R. (1972). *Rainbow Beach Recreational Area in detail.* Winnipeg: Manitoba Department of Tourism, Recreation and Cultural Affairs.

Shay, C.T. (2003). *The first Manitoba farmers: plant remains from the Lockport site.* The Prairie Garden, 131-134.

Smith, C. (1972). *The Lake St. George area: a provincial master plan for recreational use.* Winnipeg: Manitoba Department of Tourism and Recreation.

Snow Lake Chamber of Commerce. (1970). *Saga of Snow Lake.*

Somers, J.G. *History of park and recreational development on Crown lands in Manitoba 1930 - 1963.*

Stilwell, W.J. (1988). *The Baldy Mountain cabin: the history and role of forest rangers and game wardens in the Baldy Mountain area.* Manitoba Natural Resources.

Suggett, G. (1984). *Special features inventory Whiteshell Provincial Park.* Winnipeg: Manitoba Natural Resources.

Swan River Valley Historical Society. (1984). *Lasting impressions: historical sketches of the Swan River Valley.*

Teller, J.T. (Ed.). (1984). *Natural heritage of Manitoba: legacy of the ice age.* Winnipeg: Manitoba Museum of Man and Nature.

Tisdale, M.A. (1978). *Investigations at the Stott site: a review of research from 1947 to 1977.* Winnipeg: Manitoba Department of Tourism and Cultural Affairs.

Trommelen, M. & Ross, M. (2010). *Subglacial landforms in northern Manitoba, Canada based on remote sensing.* Journal of Maps, 618-638.

Trueman, D.L. (1975, Summer). *A fourth meteorite crater in Manitoba.* Manitoba Nature, 18-21.

Waldon, R.N. (1972, Spring). *The doomed dunelands.* Zoolog, 14-23.

Wilson, H. & Aykroyd, S. (1999). *Wilderness Manitoba: land where the spirit lives.* Erin, ON: Boston Mills Press.

Winnipeg Beach Moonlight Days.

Witty, D. (1969). *Paint Lake recreation area and Grass River scenic waysides.* Winnipeg: Manitoba Department of Tourism and Recreation.

Witty, D. (1971). *Proposed extension of Rocky Lake Recreation Area.* Winnipeg: Manitoba Department of Tourism and Recreation.

Also:

Departmental annual reports, 1932 to present.

Manitoba Conservation, Parks and Natural Areas Branch, park maps, campground maps, and brochures.

Manitoba newspapers at http://www.manitobia.ca.

Winnipeg Free Press Archives at http://archives.winnipegfreepress.com/

Index

Index